BOOK ACCELERATOR

*How to Write a Bestseller in 16 Weeks:
Boost Your Business, Increase Your
Income and Get Noticed!*

DAWNA STONE

Copyright © 2017 by Dawna Stone

All rights reserved. Except as permitted under the U.S. Copyright Act of 1976, no part of this publication may be reproduced, distributed or transmitted in any form or by any means, or stored in a database or retrieval system, without prior written permission of the publisher.

Printed in the United States of America

First Edition: July 2017
10 9 8 7 6 5 4 3 2 1

ISBN 978-0-9992123-0-1

Cover Design by Melissa Mellert

Edited by Corinne Whiting

Published by Bay Point Media

Formatting services provided by

Disclaimer: This book provides advice but does not guarantee any specific outcomes or results.

Trademarked names are used throughout the book. Instead of placing a trademark symbol after every occurrence of a trademarked name, we use names in an editorial fashion only, with no intention of infringement of the trademark. Where such designations appear in the book, they have been printed with initial caps.

Contents

Introduction: Is Book Accelerator For You? 3

A Blueprint for Success 7
    Chapter 1: Should You Write a Book? 9
    Chapter 2: The Book Accelerator Methodology 13

Plan 21
    Chapter 3: The Vision/Concept 23
    Chapter 4: Your Audience 29
    Chapter 5: Your Voice 33
    Chapter 6: The Book Structure 41

Write 51
    Chapter 7: The Book's Purpose 53
    Chapter 8: The Perfect Outline 57
    Chapter 9: Your Introduction 65
    Chapter 10: Developing Productive Writing Habits 67

Edit 81
    Chapter 11: Developing a Feedback Process 83
    Chapter 12: Hiring an Editor 87

Format & Design 91
    Chapter 13: Formatting Your Book 93
    Chapter 14: A Title That Sells 109

Chapter 15: A Cover That Captivates 115

Publish 121
Chapter 16: Self-Publishing vs. Traditional Publishing 123
Chapter 17: Self-Publishing 127
Chapter 18: Traditional Publishing 129

Market 133
Chapter 19: Building Pre-Launch Buzz 135
Chapter 20: Launching Your Book 143

Monetize 155
Chapter 21: Monetize Your Book 157

Conclusion 161
Chapter 22: Accountability 163

Appendix I: Self-Publishing Resources 171

Appendix II: Sample Focus Group Invite Letter 173

Sell More Copies of Your Book!

Download your FREE guide:

Find out more at BookAccelerator.com

Introduction: Is *Book Accelerator* For You?

Publishing my first book changed my life for the better. It catapulted my income, opened countless doors, landed me five-figure speaking engagements and a six-figure traditional book deal, in addition to getting me regular gigs on TV and radio shows as an expert guest—ultimately providing me with even more credibility.

I believe that anyone who wants to write a book, feels passionate about a specific topic or has expertise worth sharing should publish, but few ever get past the initial planning phase. My advice: Don't let another day go by while simply thinking about writing a book. Let Book Accelerator be your guide, with its proven step-by-step process that helps you go from the idea phase to completed book in as short as 16 weeks.

I wrote my first book—and all that have followed—by using the Book Accelerator methodology. I wrote each one while simultaneously running two companies and taking care of two young children. The Book Accelerator program provided me with a framework that kept me motivated and on track, and it will give you the tools needed to finish your book, too—no matter how busy you are or how many times you've tried before. If you're serious about writing a book and willing to give the process some time and effort, Book Accelerator is for you!

I know the Book Accelerator methodology works because I've used it to write four bestsellers. Not only did each of my books hit Amazon's bestseller list, but they also helped me cumulatively earn hundreds of thousands of dollars.

Many dream of one day writing a book, but few ever follow through. I was almost one of those well-intentioned people. I had wanted to write a book for as long as I could remember. In fact, nearly 20 years went by from the day I wrote that first word to the moment the completed project finally got published. That first year, I even got so far as to create a title, subtitle, table of contents and several chapters; but that's where I stalled. About once a year, I would take out the book's rough start and vow to dig in again. But that enthusiasm would only last for a few days before the unfinished chapters would return to that dormant computer folder titled "My Book."

It wasn't until nearly two decades passed that I figured out a program that provided the structure and motivation needed to finally follow through. As of today, I've used that same methodology to write a 60,000-word book in less than 16 weeks, both a 50,000- and 40,000-word book each in under 12 weeks and a 30,000-word book in less than six!

I've also had very different experiences with each book. I've self-published, I've received five-figure and six-figure book deals (both from large publishing houses), and, for my most recent project, I've partnered with a popular national magazine. In fact, my self-published book did so well that a large publishing house ended up giving me a lucrative deal to expand on that original concept.

I'm sharing all of this because I used the Book Accelerator methodology to make every one of my books a success, and I am confident the program can help you do the same.

Book Accelerator will:

- Teach you how to write a best-selling book in less than 16 weeks, even if you currently don't know where to begin.
- Show you how to produce a high-quality, self-published book or how to get a traditional publisher to write you a five- or six-figure advance.

- Demonstrate how to use your book as a tool to boost your business or career, increase your income, gain new clients, customers or fans and become a sought-after expert in your field.
- Provide the strategies needed to build buzz for a book launch.
- Teach you how to monetize your book, earn passive income and get paid for your valuable knowledge.
- Help you build a platform for success!

A book can be the difference between simply doing well and becoming ultra successful. Don't wait another moment to get started. Let Book Accelerator help you become a best-selling author today!

A Blueprint for Success

Chapter 1:
Should You Write a Book?

In today's fast-paced environment, I think we would all agree that finding time to do everything on one's to-do list can be extremely challenging (not to mention fitting in those important personal activities like spending time with family and friends, exercising, cooking healthy meals, sleeping and so on). So how, you may wonder, will you ever have time to write a book, too?

If you're reading this, no matter your current level of busyness you must be already contemplating writing a book. I have great news; picking up Book Accelerator is an excellent first step. But let's start with the basics: Is writing a book truly the best move for you?

I believe that, if you are: an entrepreneur who wants to grow your business; an employee who wants to take his or her career and salary to the next level; a stay-at-home mom who wants to enjoy passive income; or a leader in the community who wants to boost his or her credibility (both locally and nationally) or simply promote a cause, then becoming a published author is right for you.

For the entrepreneur…

Writing a book can be the necessary catalyst to grow your business, boost your revenues and give you the freedom of which you've only dreamt. Authoring a book—no matter how busy you may be—is something every entrepreneur should do (but very few do). Those authors who *do* follow through land in a league of their own, gaining even more influence and building more credibility.

A book can be the perfect sales and marketing tool for your business by gaining you more credibility, garnering more trust and catapulting your business to the top. The authority and prestige that accompany authoring a book can mark the difference between simply making ends meet and being profitable beyond your wildest dreams. A book is also the best possible brand builder. It can strengthen your company's brand, your personal brand or both.

Authoring a book can help build trust in the eyes of potential customers. Once you write a book on a particular subject, you immediately receive a level of trustworthiness that would otherwise be difficult to forge.

A book can also answer questions that your potential clients might have and help you close a deal before even speaking to someone—saving time and effort for everyone involved. Better yet, a book can allow you to sell your services for a premium. While more and more companies compete on price, a published book gives you the ability to hold firm on your rate. People are more willing to pay a premium to work with *the* expert, as it's naturally expected to pay more to work with the best.

For the executive…

If you work for someone or are an executive in a large company, becoming a published author can propel your career and salary, while making you an invaluable asset.

The Book Accelerator program will teach you how to write and publish a book in as short a period as 16 weeks, positively changing your life and finances in the process. You can become a sought-after speaker or someone frequently chosen to present at conferences and other industry events. All of this also makes you a valuable and more marketable asset at your current company, should you be strategizing toward a vertical move.

For the stay-at-home mom…

A book, if done correctly, can provide passive income for years. If you're a stay-at-home mom with an area of expertise or a passion you want to share, writing a book can bring in additional family income.

Depending on the topic of your book, being a published author can also help you get back into the working world, should this be a future goal. I know many extremely intelligent and hard-working women who find it difficult to re-enter the job market after taking several years off to raise their children. Being a respected, published author can open doors that otherwise might be inaccessible.

For the community leader…

If you're a leader in the community, sit on a nonprofit board of directors or have an important environmental or political message to share, a book can give you the clout to get things done and to get your cause noticed. A book that's been properly written and promoted can build awareness or make fundraising easier.

Whether you're a business owner wanting to double your revenues and profits, a seasoned executive who wants to catapult a career to the next level, a stay-at-home mom who wants to bring in passive income or a leader in the community who wants to bring awareness to a cause, publishing a book can make it happen. Book Accelerator is for you!

Chapter 2:
The Book Accelerator Methodology

The Book Accelerator Methodology is a proven and well-thought-out blueprint for writing and promoting your book. It provides a clear action plan, which eliminates the guesswork from the writing and publishing processes.

By following the step-by-step methodology, you can write and market a book in less than 16 weeks. I used this same strategy to write all four of my previously published works, and it's the process I used to write this book, too. Having a framework to follow has allowed me to create a series of bestsellers in a very short amount of time. My success proves that the Book Accelerator methodology works. I've earned more than $250,000 through my first four books; more importantly, though, in addition to this extra income, being an author has opened doors for me that would have never existed. This has led me to partnerships that otherwise wouldn't have been built, and it has enabled me to launch and grow two multi-million-dollar companies. Finishing your book and becoming a published author has the potential to do the same for you. The Book Accelerator program provides the necessary tools so that you, too, can become a successful author and reap an abundance of complementary benefits

The Book Accelerator methodology consists of seven well-defined steps. Each step, although highlighted in this chapter, will be discussed in greater detail in the chapters to come. This system, if followed correctly, will become the firm foundation upon which to write your book.

Seven-Step Book Accelerator Methodology:
1) Plan
2) Write
3) Edit
4) Format & Design
5) Publish
6) Market
7) Monetize

Step One: Plan

Proper planning is the first step in the book writing process. Most people think you can skip the planning and simply sit down and write. Although this may work for a lucky few, many get stuck or experience writer's block when trying to write without a strategy. A plan, if done correctly and thoroughly, will make the writing process simple and painless.

In step one, we will discuss the appropriate steps needed to plan for your book. These actions include vision and concept, audience, voice, and structure. This will help you focus on your message and allow you to have a clearer picture of your finished product. These steps prove crucial, as everything else that follows—from writing and marketing to monetizing your book—will stem from this initial approach. Planning before you write allows the writing portion to flow and also leads to fewer rewrites of your initial draft.

Step Two: Write

Step two will launch you into the writing process. It will help you determine the purpose of your book—an important aspect that gives a foundation for your writing and aids in future marketing. In this section, you will discover a few different techniques for building your outline. If done correctly, this makes the writing process feel effortless and straightforward. You will also learn how to properly introduce your book to hook the reader early on and how to develop productive writing habits that keep the momentum going. This is the fun part, as you get to see how everything you worked on up to this point allows for your thoughts and words to flow in a more clear and concise manner.

Step Three: Edit

In step three, you will learn the importance of feedback prior to your book's completion. I will share how to develop a focus group and how to get invaluable advice from your target audience, even if you don't know them personally. I will also discuss the editing process, how to find a talented editor and how to do the first round of edits on your own. This simple process can take your book from good to truly great!

Step Four: Format & Design

In step four, I will share 14 tips for formatting your book, and we'll discuss the importance of your book's title, subtitle and cover. The right title and cover can catapult your book to the top of the bestseller list (while a poor title or cover can negatively affect book sales and hinder discoverability). Learn how to create a total package that sells!

Step Five: Publish

In step five we will cover the pros and cons of both self-publishing and traditional publishing, and I will help you determine which method is best for you. I've been fortunate to produce both self-published and traditionally-published books, and I've found benefits to both models. I will discuss the process for each and provide constructive information needed to move forward toward the right choice.

Step Six: Market

In step six, you will learn the importance of building pre-launch buzz. Even before your book has reached completion, you should start building excitement and awareness around its release. This section will also highlight specific techniques to get the most sales from your launch. I will also share the marketing plan I used with my first self-published book—one that quickly hit the bestseller list and earned me a six-figure book deal!

Step Seven: Monetize

In the last step of the BA methodology, you will learn how to monetize your book. Although book sales are wonderful, in reality, most authors make the bulk of their money from other opportunities directly related to their book. We will discuss how you, a newly published author, can take advantage of these potential money-making alternatives.

Each of the seven steps in the Book Accelerator methodology will be covered in greater detail in future chapters, but first let's look at how each step gets incorporated into the 16-week program.

Below is the week-by-week schedule that anchors the book publishing process. Remember that this flexible schedule can be adjusted as needed. For example, if you are writing a short 15,000-word book, you may not need as many weeks for the "write" phase. If you are aiming for a much larger 50,000- to 60,000-word book, you may need to schedule some additional writing time during the "planning" phase. If, however, you are aiming to write a 20,000- to 30,000-word book, this schedule is the one to follow!

16 Week Schedule

Week 1 – Plan: Vision/Concept/Title

Week 2 – Plan: Audience/Voice/Tone

Week 3 – Plan: Structure/Problem/Solution

Week 4 – Plan: Mind Map/Diamond Map™

Week 5 – Plan: Detailed Outline

Week 6 – Write: Intro

Week 7 – Write

Week 8 – Write

Week 9 – Write

Week 10 – Write + Design Cover

Week 11 – Write

Week 12 – Write + Edit

Week 13 – Write + Edit

Week 14 – Format + Pre-Market

Week 15 – Publish + Market

Week 16 – Monetize

The Book Accelerator framework will not only teach you the step-by-step process to successfully finish your book in less than 16 weeks, but it will also show you how to produce a high-quality, self-published book or traditionally-published book that could land you a five- or six-figure book deal. It will share effective strategies for boosting your revenues and profits, gaining new customers and clients and becoming a sought-after expert in your field.

It will show you how to create buzz before you even finish your book. And once your book is complete, you will learn how to monetize the work to increase your income and improve your lifestyle.

The Book Accelerator program isn't for everyone. You must be willing to invest your time and work hard. But with my help and the seven-step Book Accelerator methodology, I have no doubt you can become a successful published author in as little as 16 weeks!

Plan

Chapter 3:
The Vision/Concept

You may have held onto a book concept for years, you may have just come up with an idea recently, or maybe you know you want to write a book, but haven't yet decided on a topic.

No matter where you land in the spectrum, settling on the concept for your book is an obvious beginning step. Yet there is one thing you should do prior to determining your topic: Establish the end goal for your book. What do I mean? You need to hone in on *why* exactly you are writing your book.

Understanding your motivation behind the book will help you come up with what you should write about. For example, if you own an insurance company and hope that publishing a book will help grow your business, you need to make sure that your chosen topic will build your authority in a crowded field. You need to provide potential clients with information this is valuable to them. Providing top-notch information will not only set you and your business apart, but it will also help you garner potential leads (and therefore clients). Keep this in mind as you determine your topic.

Answer these 12 questions to get a better understanding of why you're writing your book. Then use your answers to help conceive the best book topic possible.

1) What is your subject matter expertise?
2) What's the message you want to deliver?
3) How will the message help your reader?
4) What is your special knowledge or passion?
5) Are you writing your book to help grow your business?
6) Are you writing your book to help boost your career?
7) Do you want to go on TV and/or radio?
8) Do you want to be considered an expert in your field?
9) Do you want to use the book to build a database of potential partners/customers?
10) Do you want to become a sought-after speaker?
11) How are you qualified to provide this information?
12) Is writing this book simply for personal pleasure?

Once you've figured out why you want to write your book, it will be easier to come up with a topic that achieves your end goals.

Determining the right topic the first time around is an important piece of getting your book finished in a timely fashion. Although I often have several book ideas circulating in my mind, when it's time to move forward, my first step always involves fleshing out one particular concept. I want to make sure that I'm moving forward with a clear book topic, and I don't want to realize halfway through the book that my topic and end goal don't mesh.

One of the best ways I've found to hone in on my book topic and to ascertain that it's clear and concise is a little exercise I call the 5/3/1™ exercise. The exercise is simple but has surprisingly powerful results when getting to the core of your book concept.

Assuming you have an idea about what you want to write, I want you to spend 15 minutes describing your book in exactly five sentences. Keep reworking your thoughts until you have five well-written sentences that describe the overall concept of your book.

Once you are done with these five statements, I want you to do the same exercise, this time consolidating your thoughts to only three sentences. Although you may be tempted to simply cut out two sentences from the exercise above, I would encourage you to re-evaluate your initial, longer description to see if you can rework (into three sentences) the most important elements that best describe your book.

I'm sure you've already guessed what comes next. Once you have your three-sentence description, I want you to think of one concise sentence. Don't worry about the length of the sentence initially, but once you have a draft, try to make sure it is clear, concise and compelling. (We'll discuss these three characteristics again later when talking about your title.) In fact, this one-sentence description just may become the subtitle of your book.

Remember that your description, no matter its length, doesn't have to be perfect. You can always tweak it later. This first exercise simply gets you thinking about your topic by highlighting the most important aspects of your book. This one sentence should convey your message to your reader as simply and clearly as possible.

Here's a rough example from this book:

Five Sentences: Have you always wanted to write a book? Book Accelerator teaches you how to write your first book in less than 16 weeks. It shares the many benefits of writing a book and provides a step-by-step process for making it happen. If you're looking to build your business or boost your career or simply looking for passive income, Book Accelerator will show you how becoming a published author can help you achieve your goals. The Book Accelerator methodology makes the writing process simple, painless and fun!

Three Sentences: Have you always wanted to write a book? Book Accelerator provides all the tools needed to go from idea to printed book in less than 16 weeks. If you're looking to build your business or boost your career or simply looking for passive income, Book Accelerator will show you how becoming a published author can help you achieve your goals.

One Sentence: Book Accelerator's step-by-step process shows you how to write a book in 16 weeks, helping you boost your business, increase your income and get noticed!

Once you have your one-, three- and five-sentence descriptions, you will be better able to understand your core audience as well as determine your voice and overall book structure (all three of which we will cover next).

Chapter 4:
Your Audience

Writing a book without first understanding your audience is like writing a book and not allowing anyone to read it. If you don't know who you are writing for, you won't be able to provide your reader with what they need.

Most first-time authors make the mistake of trying to reach the largest audience possible. In reality, they will often be much more successful when catering to a smaller, well-defined audience. I learned this lesson the hard way.

In 2003 I left my job as Chief Marketing Officer of a $700-million publicly-traded company and decided to launch a national magazine. As my first foray into the world of publishing, it proved an exciting but challenging experience. The magazine, called *Her Sports*, was, as it sounds, a women's sports magazine. The magazine covered mostly individual endurance sports like running, cycling, swimming and mountain biking. The magazine did not cover any team sports like softball, basketball or tennis.

Although I thought the magazine had a niche—women interested in sports—it was often difficult to explain to people exactly which sports the publication covered. Readers would write letters and emails sharing their stories about volleyball, golf and sometimes even bowling and dance—all sports we didn't report on. People always wanted to know why we weren't covering "their" particular sport.

The magazine grew nicely, but it wasn't exactly where I had hoped it would be. And of course my husband wasn't thrilled that I had left a high-paying executive job to start a magazine that was just breaking even.

Two years into the project, we made the decision to rebrand the magazine and make the focus much more narrow. The vast majority of our content had focused on running anyway, so we rebranded the magazine as *Women's Running*. Although our overall potential audience shrunk to female runners, the magazine soared! Newsstand sales tripled with the first issue, our subscriber base more than doubled during the first year of the rebranding, and new advertisers flocked to the magazine in droves.

Eight years after launching the magazine, *Women's Running* unquestionably had become one of the top running magazines in the world; it had gained a plethora of top advertisers like Toyota, Ford, Nike, Timex, L'Oréal, Kraft, Under Armour and many others. In 2012 I sold the magazine for millions and learned a powerful and profitable lesson about the importance of finding one's niche.

It is understandable to assume that if you cut your core audience, you will lose readers; however, in reality, the opposite typically happens. When your content centers on a small but well-defined audience, your material becomes much more likely to resonate with potential readers and is therefore more attractive to them.

Once you stray from the belief that a larger audience is better, you can start thinking about who will truly benefit from your book. Target your content to a niche market, and become the authority in that specific industry or segment.

Even before I write one word of a book, I like to do a simple exercise to help discover the core audience. Before you begin, take a few minutes to answer these eight questions to better understand your readership.

1) Does your book cater to a specific gender?
2) What age range is your target audience?

3) What does your audience want/need (i.e. is there a problem to solve)?

4) Where does your potential reader live?

5) Are they married, single, do they have kids, etc.?

6) Does your reader work? Does he or she own a business or work for someone?

7) What's the average household income of your reader?

8) What are your reader's interests or passions?

Knowing who you are writing for will keep you on track and allow you to relate in a way that makes your reader desire more. And remember: Find your niche. Bigger isn't always better; when it come to writing a book, a smaller and well-defined audience can be much more lucrative.

Chapter 5:
Your Voice

Once you have a clearer understanding of your audience, you can better determine your voice. Your tone determines how the reader connects with you; it also drives the personality of your work.

Your voice is important in building a relationship with your reader. A strong tone not only establishes you as authority, but it also gives your book a distinct personality. The particular voice you choose is very dependent on your audience. For example, if you are writing a children's book, your speech would be different than if you are writing a scientific journal and different yet again if you are writing a spiritual work.

Although we are all born with unique voices, that dynamic often changes depending on who we are speaking to. I speak differently to my kids than I do to my husband (and differently yet again if I'm talking to a potential client or customer). Although there may be some consistent personality traits unique to me, the voice gets altered depending on the situation.

As you begin to plan for your book, voice will prove just as important as your vision or your concept. How do you want your readers to perceive you? How will you best connect?

Take care to address your specific audience appropriately. An ill-fitted voice can make your audience feel alienated, while a suitable voice can make readers feel engaged in your writing and instantaneously connected to you.

> *Tip:* Once you find your voice, keep it consistent. Switching back and forth from formal to informal or humorous to serious can be distracting to the reader, potentially making them feel disconnected.

It's important to remember that there is no correct or incorrect voice. But there can be the wrong voice for you or the wrong voice for your audience. For example, if I tried to be cheeky, playful and trendy, the reader would most likely see through my writing, as these three descriptors are just not my style. For others, this tone may flow perfectly and come across as extremely genuine and compelling; for me, however, it would be forced.

My writing tends to be personal, friendly and informative. Although this has proven to work for me, since it stays true to my personality, others may have found success with a humorous, mocking or sarcastic voice. Take "Thug Kitchen," for example. This unique cookbook uses slang and profanity to sell the vegan lifestyle. While this distinctive personality works well for the writer's specific niche, it most likely wouldn't work well for the larger cookbook audience. The best way to ensure you're using the "right" voice is to simply stay true to yourself and your own unique personality.

So how do you find your voice? Below is a little exercise that may help. Given the subject of your book and your audience, select the three adjectives you believe would best represent your personality and a tone effectively connecting you to your target reader.

Pick three:

- Abrasive
- Accusatory
- Arrogant
- Bitter
- Casual
- Cold
- Concerned
- Academic
- Angry
- Assertive
- Candid
- Chatty
- Comical
- Condescending

- Confrontational
- Direct
- Emotional
- Encouraging
- Enthusiastic
- Formal
- Friendly
- Impartial
- Informative
- Intimate
- Lighthearted
- Mean-spirited
- Motivational
- Optimistic
- Persuasive
- Playful
- Sarcastic
- Serious
- Sincere
- Sophisticated
- Straightforward
- Thoughtful
- Trendy
- Virtuous
- Witty
- Conversational
- Educational
- Empathetic
- Entertaining
- Factual
- Frank
- Humble
- Impersonal
- Intense
- Judgmental
- Loving
- Mocking
- Negative
- Overenthusiastic
- Pessimistic
- Righteous
- Sentimental
- Silly
- Skeptical
- Spiritual
- Sympathetic
- Tough
- Upbeat
- Whimsical

Pull out the three (or more) adjectives that best represent the personality you want for your book, and refer to them throughout the writing process.

I would be remiss if I didn't also touch on the difference between a positive and negative voice. Although plenty of authors have found success in using a negative voice, a positive voice typically sells better. The same rings true for an informal versus formal tone. Informal, as long as it is still professional, typically sells better. Save formal for research journals; your reader likely prefers to feel like you are right there with them, and being too formal is an easy was to make them feel detached. Just remember to not sound so informal that you lose credibility. You need to find a balance. An overly formal tone might make your book dry and uninteresting, but if you're *too* informal, you won't come across as an authority.

Informal---------------|----------------------------------Formal

Positive------|--Negative

Your particular voice will determine where you fall on the spectrum of informal versus formal and positive versus negative.

I'm a huge proponent of employing a positive tone. In fact, I'm absolutely adamant that any book I write comes across as uplifting. This desire to steer clear from the negative actually caused me some problems when I started working on my first book.

My first book, a business success book, had a rather quick turnaround time, as the publisher wanted to capitalize on the fact that I had recently won NBC's *The Apprentice: Martha Stewart* TV show. Since I was working full-time in New York City for Martha and also trying to run a business (my national magazine) back home, I had very limited free time. So, my agent suggested I use a ghostwriter to help write my book. I agreed. I met with several ghostwriters, reviewed their work, conducted a few phone interviews and finally selected someone who I thought would be a good match.

I visited the ghostwriter a few times in person. Each time she spent several hours recording my thoughts. I even provided a detailed outline so that nothing would be missed. A few weeks into the process, the ghostwriter sent me the first three chapters. All three were written in an extremely negative tone. I went back to our recorded interviews and confirmed that my message had been upbeat and extremely positive. The ghostwriter, however, took the liberty to write the book in a negative tone, as she felt fear would be the best motivator.

I tried to explain that she didn't capture my voice or personality in the chapters, but she insisted that fear was a better tactic than motivation. We ended up parting ways, and I scrapped everything she wrote to start over. Although ghostwriters can be a great option for the busy executive, my first experience wasn't the best. With a strict deadline looming, I had to develop a process or blueprint for writing a very long book in a very short time frame—something I am still grateful for today, as it forced me to figure out an easy and efficient book writing process. This initial book writing experience commenced what became—several books later—the methodology for Book Accelerator.

Although there is nothing wrong with using a ghostwriter, I find it much more gratifying to see a book that I've penned come to fruition. It's also a much easier way to capture your own voice and unique personality, rather than trying to convey these very personal attributes to a third party (in hopes of them capturing them). The extra effort it takes to write your own book will be well worth it in the end, and with Book Accelerator you can do it, too!

3 Tips For Finding Your Voice:

Be authentic—Don't try to copy another person's voice.

Stay positive—It's much easier to connect with your reader through a positive voice.

Be consistent—Don't go from formal to using slang, as it will confuse your reader.

Chapter 6:
The Book Structure

Once you've determined your topic and have a good understanding of your audience and voice, you're ready to determine the structure of your book. I always enjoy this stage of the process. I like envisioning what my finished book will look like, and coming up with the structure in the beginning saves you time later in the process. With my first book, a 60,000-word business book, I did most of the necessary planning, however, I didn't think much about the structure until the book had been completed. It turns out the finished manuscript was just over 45,000 words, which would have been perfect had I been self-publishing, but I had a book deal from a large publishing houses contracting me to deliver 60,000 words.

Had I planned out the structure of my book based on the word count, I would have saved myself a lot of added stress and also a great deal of time. It turns out that feeling great about a completed manuscript—only to discover you still have an additional 15,000 words to write—is an extremely depressing realization.

Although I was able to add a small amount of copy to a few chapters, the bulk of the additional word count came in the form of sidebars and text blocks. Fortunately these additional elements added value to the book and also broke up long blocks of text, ultimately making the book even more reader-friendly.

Before you begin to write, take some time to think about the structure of your book. First figure out your ideal word count. If you are self-publishing, you will have complete control over the size of your book, eliminating any worry about running short or going over your original estimate. But even if you're self-publishing, it's a good idea to come up with a target word count when planning out the structure of your book.

Let's discuss word count first, and then we can move on to additional elements like pull quotes, charts, side bars, etc.—all of which can add great value. Before you begin, you should determine if you want a paperback, hardcover or e-book. For your first book, I would suggest both a paperback and an e-book.

If you're planning to do only an e-book (as many authors do today), you can get away with a much smaller book. Many e-books on Amazon have fewer than 20,000 words and some have as few as 10,000. But since this program is about doing both a printed book and an e-book, I would suggest not going below 20,000 words (and an even better goal would be totaling somewhere between 20,000 and 30,000 words). If your book ends up over 30,000 or even 40,000-plus, that's great, but a good goal for your first book would be between 20,000 and 30,000 words.

Use the chart below to help decide on an appropriate word count for your book.

e-book	15,000-20,000 words
Small paperback	20,000-30,000 words
Bigger, more substantial paperback	30,000-45,000 words
Hardcover, full-length book	50,000-70,000 words

As I mentioned, my first book was 60,000 words, my second was 40,000, my third was 50,000 and my fourth, sold primarily as an e-book through "Shape" magazine, was just over 30,000 (31,269 before editing, to be exact).

Once you've determined your ideal length, we can develop both a writing schedule as well as a structure that makes sense. Let's use a 30,000-word book as an example. Going back to our 16-week schedule, we see that there are eight "writing weeks." So the math is simple; if we want to end up with a 30,000-word manuscript and have eight weeks to write, we need to write approximately 3,750 words a week or 750 words a day—five days a week.

Some writers like to write every day. I, however, find a five-times-a-week schedule to be more manageable. I've found that committing to write five times a week works best for me. Do whatever works best for you. We will cover the topic of scheduling time in a future chapter.

Once you've determined your book length and your weekly word count, the next step involves determining the layout of our book. I typically aim for 12 to 15 chapters, with each chapter consisting of 1,500 to 2,000 words. Once you add in your introduction, acknowledgments and any appendixes, you should end up with a solid 25,000- to 30,000-word book. Remember not to get stuck on the numbers. You can have nine chapters or 16 chapters. You can have one chapter consisting of only 1,100 words and another totaling 2,400. This is just a guide to help you get started. I've found that having a rough structure before I begin gives me a format to follow that makes the process less intimidating. But when it comes to word count and chapter length, nothing is set in stone.

In addition to word count, you should think about a few other structural variables. Once you determine whether you want a printed book, an e-book or both, you need to decide whether you want black-and-white or color interior pages. If you are doing a printed book—something that I highly recommend—you also need to determine if you want a paperback or hardcover book and if you want it printed on white or cream paper. My first book was a hardcover with black-and-white internal pages, my second was a paperback—also black-and-white pages—my third book was a 200-plus-page, full-color, hardcover cookbook (with an e-book option), and my fourth was a full-color paperback (with an e-book option, too).

Before you get started writing, you should have a vision for the structure of the book. Spend some time now to decide whether you're doing a paperback or hardcover and if your want your book to be black and white (with color cover, of course) or full color.

Note that paperback books are much more cost-effective, as is black and white versus color. For your first book—unless you're writing a children's book or cookbook—I would suggest sticking to a black-and-white paperback with an e-book option.

In addition to the cover and color choices to be made, there are a few other structural questions you should try to answer before you begin writing. Making these decisions in advance will help as you develop chapters and start the writing phase. Take some time and think about the internal pages and chapters of your book. Considering your topic, will it be necessary to use charts or graphs? Will sidebars or boxed text prove important in conveying your message? Will you utilize pull quotes, cartoons or illustrations? Below find a brief discussion about each of these structural options to help you determine whether any make sense for you to use.

Charts and graphs

Depending on your topic, charts and graphs can be extremely beneficial. I've used charts in a couple of my books as a way of providing the reader with information in an easy-to-follow format. For example, in my cookbook, I provided a 14-day eating plan; although the 14 days were spelled out in great detail in the chapters, I felt the reader would benefit from a chart highlighting each day. Think about the information provided to your reader. Will they benefit from charts or graphs, too?

Sidebars or boxed text

I've used sidebars and/or boxed text in every one of my books. This is a great technique for providing the reader with tidbits of information in a clear and concise format. It is also a great way to break up long blocks of text, which can become tedious to some readers. Think about the subject matter in your book that may benefit from the extra attention a sidebar or boxed text can provide.

Quotes or pull quotes

I love using both quotes and pull quotes, especially for a motivational or inspirational book. To get the most out of these tools and to provide value to your reader, make sure your quotes fit with the tone of your book. Pull quotes (a sentence or phrase that is pulled directly from the book content and gets written again as stand-alone text) can be valuable if you want to reiterate a specific thought. Is there something really important in a paragraph or chapter that you want the reader to focus on? Then pull it out!

Much like pull quotes, inspirational quotes can add value. I find that using quotes as openers makes the most sense and provides a positive start to chapters. But remember to only use this tool when it adds value. For example, inspirational quotes made sense for my business book and pull quotes made sense for my cookbook, but for this book, it would have appeared awkward to start each chapter with an inspirational quote.

Cartoons and illustrations

If used correctly, cartoons and illustrations can also add value to a book. However, not every topic can benefit from them and, if forced, these can negatively affect the book. If your book is lighthearted, comical and/or whimsical, cartoons could be a great addition. Or if you book requires drawings to fully communicate a concept, then illustrations may also prove beneficial.

There is no right or wrong answer when it comes to using the structural tools mentioned above, but remember that too much of a good thing can also detract from your words. For example, if you use pull quotes, do so sparingly and reiterate only those quotes from the book that will benefit the reader. The same goes with third party quotes; everyone likes inspirational quotes, but too many might overpower your message. The same rings true for illustrations. If you use them, make sure they add true value rather than simply filling up space.

When I was determining the structure of my cookbook, I found it very helpful to go to the bookstore and thumb through other books. By looking at other designs, I was able to get a feel for my likes and dislikes. I quickly realized that a simple chart could explain a weekly meal plan better than words, so I incorporated a few infographics into my cookbook. I also realized that I liked the look of pull quotes when they were done in a way that brought extra attention to a specific ingredient or dish. I also discovered that, even if it may work well for others, cartoon and/or illustrations weren't for me—at least not for any of my books to date. Pass an hour in your favorite bookstore, and find out what resonates with you. I promise the time will be well spent and you may come away with a better idea of the desired structure for your own book.

Write

Chapter 7:
The Book's Purpose

What is the purpose of your book? Most nonfiction books fall under two common areas: To help solve a problem or to teach a new skill. However, a nonfiction book can also be used to inform, to persuade or simply to entertain the reader. If you've been thinking about your topic for awhile now, you probably already know where your book falls in this spectrum.

If your nonfiction book has been designed to solve a problem or teach a new skill, a simple process will help the reader stay engrossed from start to finish.

Follow these five simple steps to ensure that your reader remains connected with your book throughout, understands the problem you're going to solve and trusts that you have the ability to help them.

Your book should:

1) **State the problem**: Be as clear and concise as possible. For your first book, I would suggest focusing on solving one problem rather than multiple. The market is changing rapidly, and people today often prefer books that focus on a niche and solve one specific issue rather than those that cover a broad range of topics. You should be able to explain the problem you set out to solve in less than three sentences. You can expand upon the problem with examples, personal experiences and so on, but the reader should be given a clear and concise description upfront of the issue at hand.

2) **Provide a solution**: Explain how your book will solve the reader's problem. Again, be as clear and concise as possible. State how the solution will help the reader. What will change, and how will his or her life improve? When possible, use personal examples, testimonials and research.

3) **Provide evidence for your solution**: Testimonials, research and scientific studies give the reader added confidence in your approach. Offer the reader a reason to believe that your solution will work by providing concrete evidence.

4) **State why your solution is the best solution**: Show how your solution stands out among others on the

market. Remember, no matter your topic, there are more than likely several other books covering a similar theme. My first book explored business success. As you can imagine, thousands of similar books already exist on this very broad topic, so I needed to explain to the reader why my approach was the best approach. The same applied to my second, third and fourth books—all were healthy eating/weight-loss books, which happen to belong to a very crowded field in the publishing market. Let the reader know what sets your book apart and why your book excels above the rest.

5) **Convince your readers that they've made the right choice in purchasing your book**: If you did a good job with steps one through four, step five simply involves restating the previous steps and getting the reader excited about reading on.

A book that teaches a new skill can follow a very similar plan. Explain the skill that readers will learn and why it is important for them, walk them through the learning process, share examples of how the skill has helped others and provide evidence that your book excels beyond others in teaching this particular skill. Then restate why purchasing your book was the right choice.

If you are clear and concise about your book's purpose, you are more likely to keep your readers' attention and even prompt them to purchase (and even recommend) your book to others.

Take a few minutes to write down your book's purpose. Then carefully review steps one through five above and state in a few sentences how your book achieved each goal. This simple exercise will help you begin the writing process.

Chapter 8:
The Perfect Outline

Although there might not be such a thing as the perfect outline, a strong one can make a huge difference in how quickly you're able to write your book. Additionally, a detailed outline can mark the difference between a painful writing experience and an enjoyable one.

Many different strategies exist when it comes to writing your book, and the most important factor involves finding the method that works best for you. What may work for one person, may not work for another.

For most people, trying to come up with a book outline proves the most difficult part of the process. Most of us don't know where to begin or how to flesh out a concept in a way that makes sense and allows the book to move towards a structure that flows smoothly from chapter to chapter.

If you haven't yet attempted to write a book or if you've tried and didn't succeed in following through, I would suggest using one of three approaches to help you get started—mind mapping, Diamond Mapping™ or card outlining.

Mind Mapping

Although effective for many writers, this process can become messy and sometimes overwhelming, allowing your thoughts to pour onto a page without any formal structure. Mind mapping is synonymous with brain dumping. It's a way for the writer to get all of his or her ideas onto paper without worrying about the arrangement. I like that this approach gives writers a freedom that aids idea generation. Mind mapping has no rules and no "wrong" ideas, topics or concepts, but be forewarned that doing this type of brain dump can feel a little messy and chaotic. If you are someone who likes order and gets frazzled by disorganization, mind mapping may cause you a bit of anxiety. But if you're okay with a bit of temporary chaos, a mind mapping exercise can be very beneficial.

There is no correct way to mind map, but coming up with your main topic and the subtopics for your book is a good start. Place the main topic of your book in the center of a large piece of paper, and draw a circle around it. From that circle draw lines to several other circles. These will become the subtopics of your book and may become your book chapters. Take each of those circles and from them, build branches with additional thoughts, topics or keywords (any information you want to cover in that section). You can continue the process by building out additional branches from the initial branch until all your thoughts are on the page. When finished, you have what may initially look like a huge jumble of circles and branches, but if you have the patience to organize the thoughts, you will have a great start to your detailed outline.

Diamond Mapping™

Diamond Mapping™ is similar to mind mapping, yet it provides a cleaner process that follows a clear path from idea to detailed outline with little effort. The goal of Diamond Mapping™ allows you to capture your thoughts and ideas with ease.

Diamond Mapping™

_____
(Book Title Goes Here)

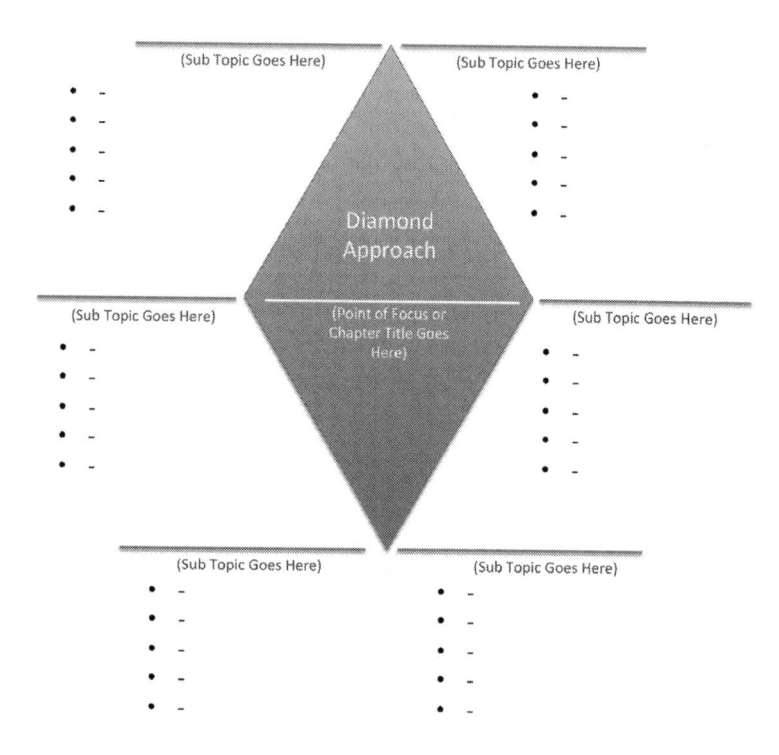

(Sub Topic Goes Here)
- -
- -
- -
- -
- -

(Sub Topic Goes Here)
- -
- -
- -
- -
- -

Diamond Approach

(Sub Topic Goes Here)
- -
- -
- -
- -
- -

(Point of Focus or Chapter Title Goes Here)

(Sub Topic Goes Here)
- -
- -
- -
- -
- -

(Sub Topic Goes Here)
- -
- -
- -
- -
- -

(Sub Topic Goes Here)
- -
- -
- -
- -
- -

Note: The above diagram shows one subtopic, which will likely become one of your book's chapters. Note: the diamond approach can have as many or as few pages as needed with each subtopic/chapter getting it's own page.

Unlike the free-flowing mind map, Diamond Mapping™ has more of a structure. With this process, you take your main topic or book title and place it at the top of the page. Then in the center of the diamond, place your subtopics. As with mind mapping, these subtopics may become your book chapters. For each subtopic, you then drill down one step further and build out areas of focus within that topic. The Diamond Map allows you take it even further and put additional thoughts or keywords under each area of focus. Each subtopic or chapter would have its own diamond page (if not more). I'm partial to Diamond Mapping™ as the process is very similar to mind mapping but it allows me to keep all my thoughts organized and allows me to go easily from my map to my detailed outline.

If you have the time and energy to put in a little extra effort, you could do both mind mapping and Diamond Mapping™. In that case, you would start with the mind map, later using it to create your Diamond Map™. From there, you would develop your detailed book outline. The benefit of doing both? You spend more time thinking about the contents of your book, which may lead to fewer revisions along the way and ultimately less time writing your book. As mentioned above, mind mapping and Diamond Mapping™ are very different, and you may feel much more comfortable with one than the other. If you are very creative, visual and don't mind things being in disarray before they begin to make sense, mind mapping could be your best choice. If, however, you're less visual and prefer lists and structure, then Diamond Mapping™ may be more up your alley. Do whichever works best for you.

Card Outlining

I realize I may take some flak for sharing this option, but I still find that this super low-tech approach of using index cards still works best for me. I love this approach, as I find reorganizing my ideas and the flow of the chapters becomes extremely manageable with the use of index cards. Simply take all your main topics and write them on individual index card. Separate them on a table or counter. Next take your subtopics and write them on another set of cards (one card for each thought or idea). Put those cards under the appropriate subtopics. I like to take it several steps further by writing high-level content on the cards and placing them in corresponding piles. Sometimes I write the exact sentences that later get transferred into the book, but more often than not, the index cards simply include ideas that I want to research and/or expand upon.

I know it may seem elementary to use index cards, but this approach has helped me write 40,000- to 60,000-word books in less than 12 weeks—something I don't believe would have been feasible with any other approach.

No matter which approach you choose, remember that outlines are living documents—meaning that nothing is ever set in stone. For many, the fear of heading in the wrong direction or not covering the right subtopics prevents them from moving forward. However, an outline, no matter how high-level or how detailed, can and should be manipulated and tweaked throughout the entire process. I don't believe I've ever stuck with my initial outline. As I begin the writing process, I always seem to delete and add chapters or shift the order. Don't let the idea that you're stuck with your first outline hold you back from getting it done. Think of your first outline attempt as a rough draft that will be perfected throughout the process.

Chapter 9:
Your Introduction

The introduction can become the most important part of your work. If your book is sold in bookstores, it's usually the first place people glance when deciding what to buy.

If you have a book or e-book for sale on Amazon, the introduction almost always gets included in the "Look Inside" preview, visible to potential readers before purchases. And even if you're giving away your book, it's most likely the introduction that gets your reader to continue on.

A solid introduction provides the reader with enough detail to solidly understand what the book covers, how the information will be structured and how it will be of benefit.

Many writers struggle with their introduction. They don't know how much detail to provide, how many words to use or which points to cover. Over the years, I've come up with a strategy that has made writing the introduction a quick and simple process.

Follow the six steps below to build a strong and engaging introduction:

1) Connect with readers by identifying a problem or concern and letting them know you understand the issue (or issues) at hand.

2) Offer a solution to the problem—one that has been proven effective. And let readers know how you will provide the solution, i.e. tips, tools, framework, etc.

3) Provide an explanation for why you are qualified to disseminate this information/solution.

4) State how the book will help the reader or change his or her life for the better (providing a bullet list of benefits works well).

5) Highlight each section in the book to give the reader a feel for what's to come.

6) Restate the problem, and make a claim or promise to the reader.

Once you have this process down, the introduction becomes a rather easy endeavor and can prove your best sales tool.

Chapter 10:
Developing Productive Writing Habits

In this section, we will discuss writing habits while developing a personalized plan that works with your specific schedule and lifestyle. This plan will help you stay on track and will also teach you how to write on a consistent basis.

If you remember, in chapter two we developed a timeline for each stage of the Book Accelerator methodology. I've put that timeline on the following page for quick reference.

16 Week Schedule

Week 1 – Plan: Vision/Concept/Title

Week 2 – Plan: Audience/Voice/Tone

Week 3 – Plan: Structure/Problem/Solution

Week 4 – Plan: Mind Map/Diamond Map™

Week 5 – Plan: Detailed Outline

Week 6 – Write: Intro

Week 7 – Write

Week 8 – Write

Week 9 – Write

Week 10 – Write + Design Cover

Week 1 – Write

Week 12 – Write + Edit

Week 13 – Write + Edit

Week 14 – Format + Pre-Market

Week 15 – Publish + Market

Week 16 – Monetize

The next step involves taking weeks six through thirteen from the schedule above and drilling down one more level to develop a writing schedule for those eight weeks. At this point, and with the help of chapter six, I hope you've narrowed down your target book length. Remember that this number isn't set in stone. When I first sat down to write *Book Accelerator*, I developed my writing scheduled based on 20,000 words, but the book ended up totaling closer to 25,000. The word count goal simply provides a gauge for helping plan out your daily/weekly writing schedule.

For the purpose of this exercise, let's assume your word count goal is 25,000 words. Not only does this seem to be a manageable book length, but I also think it's the sweet spot for a self-published book—especially for a first-time author.

Given this word count goal, I would recommend a writing goal of 1,000 words a day, five days a week. Why only five days a week? I know many authors are adamant about putting pen to paper every day to keep up the habit of writing. But as a mom with two kids and two companies to run, I found that the five-days-a-week goal works well for me. I schedule my writing for Monday through Friday and take the weekend off to spend with my family. However, if something keeps me from achieving my weekday writing goals, I know I have the weekend to catch up on my word count. This flexibility works extremely well for me and can alleviate some of the pressure many writers feel when trying to adhere to a strict daily schedule.

You may think that 1,000 words a day, done five days a week, will help you complete your draft in five weeks (rather than the eight weeks allotted in the Book Accelerator methodology). This is intentional, as you'll more than likely need to rewrite sections of the book. I've been known to cut entire chapters from my manuscript or to add in unplanned chapters. The eight-week writing schedule gives you the time needed to rework your book and make any necessary changes, deletions or additions along the way.

Let's look at five simple steps to make the writing process much more manageable.

1) Set writing goals.
2) Schedule your writing.
3) Make your writing a priority.
4) Develop a writing ritual.
5) Just write!

Set writing goals

I've always been a huge proponent of goal setting. I set exercise goals, weight loss goals and revenue goals for my businesses. I truly believe that establishing and tracking objectives has played a huge part in my success. I've even done TV segments on goal setting and have written multiple articles on the subject. In fact, I once dedicated an entire hour-long radio show to the topic. So when it came time to write my first book, you can imagine that goal setting topped my to-do list.

Not sure how to set or achieve your writing goals? Follow these nine steps:

1) **Clearly define your goal**: Your goal should be well defined and given an assigned time frame. Daily or weekly objectives typically work best for writers.

2) **Make it realistic**: Your goal should be challenging but also achievable. Make sure you set yourself up for success, not failure.

3) **Write it down**: Put your goal on paper or in a computer file, and refer to it often. The simple act of writing something down makes it real.

4) **Make sure it's "your" goal**: Just because your favorite author writes 5,000 words a day or spends eight consecutive hours at his or her computer, doesn't

mean the same will work for you. Make sure the goal you set is based on your schedule, not someone else's.

5) **Break it down into smaller steps**: Having a goal of writing 25,000 words seems much less attainable than a goal of writing 5,000 words a week or even 1,000 words a day. Set milestones or short-term goals that will keep you on track and help keep you motivated.

6) **Review your goals**: Track your progress on a regular basis. Praise yourself for staying on track. If you happen to fall off, take the necessary steps to get back on schedule.

7) **Share it with others**: Simply telling someone else about your ambitions causes you to feel more accountable. Let everyone around you know you're writing a book.

8) **Adjust as needed**: Goals rarely unfold exactly as we plan. Be prepared to reevaluate your goals and make adjustments along the way.

9) **Reward yourself**: Sticking to your plan can take a great deal of effort. Reward yourself for a job well done. It doesn't matter how big or small the reward, just acknowledge your hard work.

Decide if you are going to set daily or weekly goals. I do both. To clarify, I keep a weekly goal—say 5,000 words a week—and a daily goal of 1,000 words a day, five days a week. The reason I do both daily and weekly goals? I know that there will be times when I may not be able to adhere to my daily goal and, although I try very hard to achieve that quota, I allow some flexibility as long as I hit my weekly goal. So if I can't write my 1,000 words on Wednesday, I know I can make up for it later in the week or even during the weekend.

This type of goal setting works best for me, but you will need to find what works best for you. If you have a busy schedule, allowing yourself to keep weekly goals may give you the flexibility you need. I know from experience that unexpected distractions arise, and having weekly goals allows me to front-load my writing when necessary. If you are new to writing and uncertain what will work best for you, I would suggest following my lead and setting both a daily and weekly goal; you can then adjust as needed.

Schedule your writing

Your writing schedule will most likely be based on the word count goals you set for yourself. But no matter if you set daily or weekly writing goals, you will need to schedule time to achieve those goals.

The biggest roadblock writers face often involves simply finding time to write. This is why scheduling your writing time becomes crucial to achieving your goals. We schedule dentist appointments, lunch meetings, conference calls and other important events into our calendar; writing should be no different. I set a one- or two-hour writing block five days a week and I schedule these writing sessions just like I would any other important meeting. If you want to achieve your writing goals, you need to schedule your writing!

Make writing a priority

Make your book writing a priority, just like you would any important meeting, conference call or lunch date. It's one thing to set word count goals, but it's another to carve out specific hours during your day for writing.

Although establishing a set time each day would be advantageous, I realize this may not be realistic for everyone. If possible, however, I would suggest dedicating the same hours every day to writing. I know writers who love working first thing in the morning, while many night owls find that ideas flow best when the rest of the family is fast asleep in bed. Find a time that works best for you.

I've toyed with having a set one- to two-hour window every day, but my schedule realistically doesn't allow it.

My writing schedule tends to vary each day, but I still schedule it into my calendar at the start of each week and rarely deviate from the plan. For example, every Monday my daughter has evening gymnastics so I have a full hour of uninterrupted writing time while waiting at her studio. Although it's extremely loud and I have to work on a plastic picnic table, I find that I write really well during that hour—often even better than in the quiet of my own home or office.

In addition to that set hour each Monday, I typically schedule two writing lunches. There is a great Italian restaurant in my office building, and on a regular basis I commandeer a table in the eatery's bar area . The staff knows me by name, and the food is great. I write for a minimum of one hour during those scheduled lunch writing sessions, but I've been known to continue for as long as two hours. These writing lunches are set in my schedule and planned in advance, just like any other important lunch appointment.

Since I'm not a full-time author and I also have two companies to run, I have to be somewhat flexible with my writing time. Yet I still almost always manage to set aside at least an hour or two each day. Sometimes that means waking up an hour early, spending my lunch hour writing or working at night after my kids have gone to sleep.

Once you come up with a plan that works for you, put it in your calendar and stick to it!

> **If you're having trouble making your writing a priority, try asking yourself these four questions:**
>
> 1) What must I get done today?
>
> 2) What doesn't need to be done?
>
> 3) What can wait?
>
> 4) What can I delegate?

Develop a writing ritual

Now that you have your writing scheduled into your day or week, it's advantageous to come up with a work-time ritual. If you are able to find a set place to write, you can easily develop established habits that will help you get in a creative mood.

I don't often write at home, but when I do, I use a wonderful nook that is bright and spacious. I like to brew a cup of black tea, set out all my papers and notes alongside my computer and develop a comfortable writing environment.

Simply establishing a writing routine can make the process much more enjoyable. Also, if done consistently, this ritual can help turn your writing into a habit—making it much easier to adhere to a schedule. And once you develop strong writing patterns, you will no longer feel overwhelmed by the writing process. Develop a ritual that feels comfortable and that inspires you to write.

Just write

I know it's easier said then done, but sometimes the act of getting words down on paper proves more important than the words themselves. When writing your draft, perfection doesn't necessarily mean more success.

If you're having trouble writing or, as my nine-year-old says, you're suffering from "writer's blog" (I keep telling her it's "block…"), allow yourself to do some free writing. Simply jotting down thoughts without any intention of keeping what you produce can feel liberating. When free writing, you don't censor yourself. You don't overthink; instead you write whatever comes to mind. This flow of thoughts can become a great tool for collecting information or initially getting the writing juices flowing. Start this exercise with a short five- or 10-minute session. You may be surprised to find that a short free writing session eliminates your writer's block.

Having trouble building out your chapters? A great, helpful exercise involves asking three questions related to the chapter content. Not sure what questions to ask? Ask a friend, family member or co-worker to read your chapter and come up with three queries based on what they read. Your next steps in building out the chapter can be rooted in simply answering these questions. Not only will the exercise help you flesh out your chapters, but it will help ensure your readers get the answers they desire.

Feeling stuck on a specific section or chapter in your book? Some writing coaches suggest not deviating from the order of your outline. I strongly disagree, as I rarely write chapter one first, followed directly by chapter two, then chapter three and so on. If you get stuck, move on to another chapter. There is no set rule in regards to the order in which you must write.

I believe that the best order in which to produce your book, is the order you find the easiest and most motivational. Below is the order in which I wrote Book Accelerator. As you can see, I jumped around a lot. If I was struggling with a certain chapter, I skipped it and returned at a later date. I also wrote the chapters that I was most excited about first, as this jump-started the process and inspired me to write more.

- ✔ Introduction
- ✔ Chapter 1
- ✔ Chapter 4
- ✔ Chapter 5
- ✔ Chapter 3
- ✔ Chapter 2
- ✔ Chapter 16
- ✔ Chapter 18
- ✔ Chapter 7
- ✔ Chapter 8
- ✔ Chapter 11
- ✔ Chapter 22
- ✔ Chapter 9
- ✔ Chapter 10
- ✔ Chapter 6
- ✔ Chapter 17
- ✔ Chapter 12
- ✔ Chapter 21
- ✔ Chapter 14
- ✔ Chapter 15
- ✔ Chapter 13
- ✔ Chapter 19
- ✔ Chapter 20
- ✔ Chapter 23

I skipped around quite a bit and felt completely comfortable doing so. I don't see the benefit of struggling with a chapter that isn't flowing. I believe you should move on and come back later. More often than not, when I return to a challenging chapter, the struggle disappears and the writing suddenly flows.

Don't let some arbitrary order hold you back. Just because the book structure and chapters need to flow for the reader doesn't mean you have to necessarily write them in that order.

Remember, procrastination is the killer of dreams. Just get started. Don't be too critical of your writing, and let it naturally evolve. You will have plenty of time to alter and edit your work once you have a first draft. Let's write!

Edit

Chapter 11:
Developing a Feedback Process

Through the years, I've learned a great deal about getting feedback for my books. A large publishing house published my first book, so I had a team of people providing valuable edits throughout the entire book writing process. Since I self-published my second book, I didn't have the luxury of a team working with me on the manuscript, so I needed to find another way to obtain constructive criticism. By developing my own formal process, I was able to secure a plethora of helpful feedback.

You can always ask your family, friends or spouse for feedback, but they may feel obligated to provide only positive feedback. In reality, constructive criticism proves the most valuable tool and promises to make your book truly better.

Obtaining feedback proves so crucial that I felt compelled to put together my own focus group. The group consisted of a small number of friends who I trusted would provide honest thoughts as well as a small number of strangers. The individuals I didn't know came recommended by friends or friends of friends. I set a date for an in-person focus group and provided a draft of the manuscript to each person. Since everyone lived locally, the majority of the manuscripts could be hand-delivered.

I gave the group two weeks to read the draft and asked that they take detailed notes. I provided a list of things to consider while reading the book. The group then met for two hours to discuss the book. Before jumping into an open discussion, each person was asked to spend the first 20 to 30 minutes of the meeting answering a questionnaire. This allowed me to gather feedback prior to the open discussion and also eliminated the worry of potentially getting only "group think" (when the desire for conformity causes people to limit their feedback or to only provide feedback also offered by others, as not to go against the group's consensus).

Following the open discussion, the group enjoyed a round of drinks and appetizers as a "thank you" for their time. Each person also received a signed copy of my book when it came out and was mentioned in my acknowledgments at the front of the book.

In Appendix II I've shared a copy of the email invitation that I sent out to build interest in the focus group.

Although the focus group wasn't too costly, some expenses are associated with printing out manuscripts and providing food and drinks for your guests. If you don't have a budget, you can get similar feedback by hosting a private Facebook group or doing the entire process virtually rather than in person. In fact, I've now done variations of this focus group for my other books. Although that initial focus group was the most formal, I've found I can get equally effective feedback by doing everything online—without the need for an in-person gathering.

I've also gone straight to my social media following for feedback. Although I don't provide the manuscript to my followers (they're the ones I hope will purchase the book), I've found that simply asking them about a certain topic or chapter can yield a great deal of feedback.

Although organizing a focus group involves some hard work, I believe the feedback you receive far outweighs any time or effort expended. Use focus groups—virtual or in-person—for all aspects of your book including the content, title and cover. Trust me: Your book will be better for it!

Chapter 12:
Hiring an Editor

If you have a publishing deal, you may be provided an editor at no cost to you. That editor typically will be an on-staff member of the publishing house or will be outsourced by them to work on your book. But times are changing, and some publishing companies now expect to receive your manuscript with at least one round of edits already completed by a professional.

If you are self-publishing a book, it's imperative that you hire a book editor. Your book is your calling card, and a document full of typos, run-on sentences or other grammatical mistakes will reflect poorly on you.

Although professional editing can be expensive, more and more options exist than ever before, and many of them are quite affordable. A freelance book editor can help polish your work and, more often than not, will also provide invaluable feedback on items like clarity, flow, etc.

Some first-time authors resist hiring an editor. They are often concerned about the cost and also wonder about the necessity. They lack an appreciation for what an editor can do for them and their book. I will tell you that getting my books edited by a professional is one of the most rewarding parts of the process. I love the fact that I can send my manuscript to a professional book editor and receive unbiased and invaluable feedback—something that's difficult to get from friends and family. Not to mention, the edited version of my book is always a step up from the unedited version.

What will you pay? You can pay anywhere from $35 to $100 an hour (or more). Ask the editor not only for the hourly rate but also for a prediction of how long the work will take, based on your word count. You may also want to ask for a not-to-exceed maximum cost. And initially, if your editor hasn't come highly recommended by someone you know, it may be smart to first ask if he or she is willing to edit two or three chapters to make sure you like their style and find value in their work before proceeding. A good editor will be open to this "test."

Tips for hiring an editor

- Find an editor who specializes in nonfiction.
- Chose an editor even before your manuscript has been completed.
- Provide only a few chapters initially to make sure you and your editor are a good fit.
- Ask about an hourly rate versus a project rate, and see which option makes sense for you.
- If your editor uses an hourly rate, ask for an estimate based on your word count. Also ask the editor to keep you posted on his or her hours so you don't run over.
- Even if using an hourly rate, see if the editor would be willing to set a max rate, should the editing process take longer than expected (i.e. $65 an hour up to a $650 max, even if he or she spends more than 10 hours on the project).

Tips for finding an editor

Finding an editor your first time around can be stressful. Spending money on a service that you haven't used before or an editor you haven't worked with can be nerve-racking. To make the process less anxiety-inducing, follow these suggestions:

- Find writer/author groups on social media, and ask for recommendations.

- Ask the editor to provide several references, and take the time to actually contact individuals who the editor has previously worked with.

- Ask the editor to send you a list of books they have edited. Often Kindle will allow you to download a small sample of the book for free, which will give you a feel for the editor's work.

- Send the editor two or three chapters of your book to edit prior to hiring to get a feel for his or her editing style.

- Use an editor that works for your self-publishing platform (i.e. CreateSpace has editing services available). These individuals have already been vetted by the company and make a living as professional editors.

Hiring an editor is one of the most important things you can do for your book. If you can afford it, hire someone with book editing experience. If you simply don't have a budget for a professional editor, make sure you enlist more than one friend, family member, English major or other eligible candidate to edit your book. I can't stress enough how important it is to hire a professional. If you can afford to spend a few extra dollars on your book, this is an excellent place to invest.

Format & Design

Chapter 13:
Formatting Your Book

Assuming you are writing nonfiction, you should follow several formatting rules in order to create a professional-looking book. Although I will try to provide a comprehensive list below, I would also recommend that you read the guidelines provided by the self-publishing service you decide to use. For example, if you plan to use CreateSpace, they have a downloadable PDF submission specification that will walk you through the process for formatting your book, should you be doing it on your own.

Even if you're having someone else format your book or you hire a formatting service, you should still be familiar with the standard rules. Below find some helpful tips for a smooth book formatting process and a professional-looking finished product.

Book Size

All four of my previous books have been different sizes. I chose the size for my self-published book, but my publishers made the determination for my other books (with some input from me). When it comes time to format your book, you'll have to first select your book size. For example, CreateSpace has 12 industry-standard trim sizes for black-and-white books and seven industry-standard trim sizes for color books. Although there are many sizes to choose from, 5.25x8 and 6x9 remain the most common. I suggest doing some research. Check out books that you've purchased in the past, or go to your local bookstore to look at which sizes resonate best with you and your topic.

When I was developing my first ever cookbook, my publisher told me to spend time in the bookstore looking at other bestselling cookbooks. I spent an entire day sitting on the floor at my local Barnes & Noble, with stacks of popular cookbooks surrounding me. Not only did I determine the size that I liked best, but I was also able to share other thoughts with my publisher on color schemes, chapter headlines, photo usage, cover designs, etc. I must have taken nearly 50 pictures that I later showed my publisher to clarify my likes and dislikes. Take the time to know what you want.

Block Paragraphs

For nonfiction books, always use block paragraphs. Block paragraphs are both left- and right-aligned with a space between paragraphs. If you want, you can still choose to indent your first sentence in the paragraph. For example:

Block paragraph with no indention

This is a block paragraph with no indentions. This is a block paragraph with no indentions. This is a block paragraph with no indentions. This is a block paragraph with no indentions. This is a block paragraph with no indentions. This is a block paragraph with no indentions. This is a block paragraph with no indentions.

This is a block paragraph with no indentions. This is a block paragraph with no indentions. This is a block paragraph with no indentions. This is a block paragraph with no indentions. This is a block paragraph with no indentions. This is a block paragraph with no indentions. This is a block paragraph with no indentions.

Block paragraph with indentions

    This is a block paragraph with indentions. This is a block paragraph with indentions. This is a block paragraph with indentions. This is a block paragraph with indentions.

This is a block paragraph with indentions. This is a block paragraph with indentions. This is a block paragraph with indentions.

This is a block paragraph with indentions. This is a block paragraph with indentions. This is a block paragraph with indentions. This is a block paragraph with indentions. This is a block paragraph with indentions. This is a block paragraph with indentions. This is a block paragraph with indentions.

I tend to like block paragraphs without indentions; however, two of my three books that were traditionally published by large publishing companies used block paragraphs with indentions. It's your choice whether you use indentions or not , but definitely stick to paragraphs that are left- and right-aligned i.e. blocked.

Be Consistent

Choose one style, and stick to it. In order to have a professional-looking book, you need consistency. For example, if you use bullet points throughout your book, don't use round dots for some and diamond shapes for others. And if you use numbered lists, don't follow some numbers with periods and others with parentheses. Pick your style:

1. Use a period after the number

1) Or use a parenthesis after the number

- Use a circle for your bullet point

- Or use a diamond (or other shaped) bullet point

Just remember to be consistent throughout the book. The same goes for underlining, pull quotes, headings, subheadings, etc.

I tend to initially write without thinking too much about the consistency, as I don't want the layout or style to slow down my creative flow. I do, however, later have to go back through the manuscript to make sure I've been consistent throughout the book. Making sure the content remains uniform doesn't take too much effort, but you would be surprised how simple inconsistencies can scream "amateur." Take the time to make sure your book looks professional by staying consistent in your style.

No Double Spacing at the End of a Sentence

Back when I was in high school, we were taught to always double-space after a sentence. I know I'm giving away my age, but we did this because we were using typewriters, which used monospace fonts versus proportional fonts. This meant that, whether you typed an "M" or an "I," the letters were given the same amount of space. Typewriters didn't adjust for the letters' size difference, so two spaces after the sentence was the norm. But today's word processing software uses proportional fonts, meaning that an "M" gets more space than an "I." Today only one space is needed after a sentence; in fact, this is now the rule for typesetting. If you use two spaces in between sentences, not only will it look unprofessional, but most editors will have to make the changes in your manuscript. This habit was hard for me to break, but now I don't even think twice. One space has become my new norm.

If, like me, you learned the two-space rule and are having trouble adjusting your ways, there is an easy fix. Simply use your "find and replace" tool. Put two blank spaces into the "find" bar and one blank space into the "replace" bar. Hit enter, and the computer will take every double space and convert it to a single space. (Go to: Edit – Find – Replace)

One File vs. Many

When you're ready to upload your file to your self-publishing platform, you want to have only one file. I know some authors like to have each book chapter saved as a separate file. I have actually been known to do this if my book is more than 30,000 words, so that I can easily send off individual chapters to my editor. This way I can continue to work on some chapters while others are being edited. I can also keep track of what has been edited and what hasn't. For example, I like to change my file name from "Book_Accelerator_Ch_4.doc" to "Book_Accelerator_Ch_4_edited.doc." This allows me to monitor each chapter before and after editing. I've been known to take it one step further and save the final version as "Book_Accelerator_Ch_4_Final.doc," as I don't always accept all of my editor's corrections (although I do accept most). I know that this "final" version includes edits from my editor but also has been proofed a final time by me and is ready to publish. Once I have all my chapters in their final version, I then make sure to combine them into one document, with each chapter separated by a page break.

Use the Right Font

Font selection isn't the time to get creative. You can get imaginative with your cover, but keep it simple when it comes to your typeface. Some of the fonts I have used in previous books include Garamond, Minion and Palatino—all of which I really liked. All have slight differences but are extremely reader-friendly. If you're uncertain which font to use, you can't go wrong with one of these three. Some other common fonts for your book's typeface might be Janson, Caslon and Verdana. If you want to try more, I suggest formatting a few pages with your desired font to see what you think before making your final selection.

Font Size

A font that is too small can make your book difficult to read, and a font that is too big can make your book look unprofessional. Stick with a standard font size—typically 12pt for internal text and 18pt to 24pt for headings.

Right-Hand Start

Each new chapter should start on a right-hand page. If your chapter ends on a right-hand page, instead of starting your next chapter on the next page (a left-hand page), keep the left-hand page blank and start your chapter on the right. Note: Some publishers don't follow this rule, but I think the right-hand start rule makes for a much cleaner look. It will be up to you whether or not you want to follow this rule. Depending on how many chapters you have and where each chapter ends, this rule can add several pages to your book, which can be positive or negative. It can look impressive to have more pages, but this can also lead to higher printing costs. Check out your favorite books and authors' works, and note for yourself whether or not you want to follow this rule. Other blank pages include those opposite the inside front cover, the table of contents, the foreword and the acknowledgements. Note: This rule is for print books only.

Utilize Your Self-Publishing Platform's Formatting Service

If you have the money to hire an expert to format your book, I highly suggest doing so. In fact many of the self-publishing platforms provide these services at a reasonable cost. Kindle Direct Publishing charges $149 to $349 to format your e-book, and CreateSpace charges $249 to $349 to format your print book. Although this isn't cheap, it can save you a great deal of time and headache. If you want to save the money and format your own book, just make sure to read the guidelines for your specific self-publishing platform before getting started. If you choose to do it on your own, know that the first time will be the most time-consuming; once you have the process down, however, it will get much easier should you decide to write any future books.

Get a Sample

Once your book has been formatted and uploaded, make sure you get a sample before marketing or making your work available. It's imperative to have both a print and an e-book version to review. Too often we find mistakes that only show up when looking at the final layout. Spend the few additional dollars and extra week or so to review the final version of your book and to ensure it was formatted correctly.

Headers and Footers

Your book title and page number should appear on even pages (left) and chapter name and page number on odd pages (right). Headers are on every page with the exception of the copyright page, title page, dedication page, table of contents, foreword, acknowledgements, introduction and each chapter title page. And of course, no headers or footers appear on blank pages. You can also choose to do only headers, only footers or both. As long as you stick to the basic rule (book title on the left and chapter title on the right), you can determine whether you want to use only headers, only footers or a combination. Although I don't always get to choose, when it is up to me, I prefer to use only headers (but this is simply my personal preference).

Title Page

Your book will have two title pages. First, there's the actual cover of the book, whether hardcover, paperback or e-book. Then there will be a secondary title page that has less design elements, but instead announces the title, subtitle and author's name. The text should be centered on a right-hand page with no headers or footers. If your book has a foreword, the author of the foreword can be included right after your name (i.e. "Foreword by…."). If you have a traditional publisher, the imprint name will also be included on this page. The inside covers from two of my books can be seen on the following pages.

the healthy you diet

The 14-Day Plan for Weight Loss with 100 Delicious Recipes for Clean Eating

Dawna Stone

RODALE

JUNK FOOD FUNK

THE 3-, 5-, AND 7-DAY JUNK FOOD DETOX
FOR WEIGHT LOSS AND BETTER HEALTH

BY DAWNA STONE

meredith

© Meredith Corp. 2016. All rights reserved.

Copyright page

Your book should always include a copyright page. This typically means a left-hand page immediately following your internal cover page that includes the following information: Copyright symbol, date and author name, publisher name and address, edition, disclaimer, ISBN and publisher logo. See samples from these same two books below.

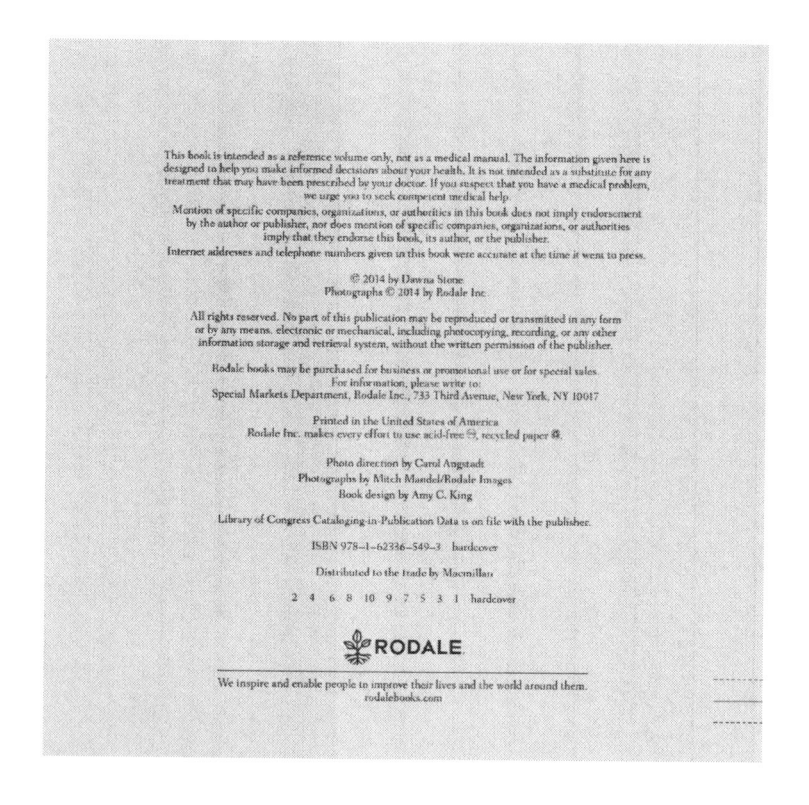

This book is intended as a reference volume only, not as a medical manual. The information given here is designed to help you make informed decisions about your health. It is not intended as a substitute for any treatment that may have been prescribed by your doctor. If you suspect that you have a medical problem, we urge you to seek competent medical help.

Mention of specific companies, organizations, or authorities in this book does not imply endorsement by the author or publisher, nor does mention of specific companies, organizations, or authorities imply that they endorse this book, its author, or the publisher.

Internet addresses and telephone numbers given in this book were accurate at the time it went to press.

© 2014 by Dawna Stone
Photographs © 2014 by Rodale Inc

All rights reserved. No part of this publication may be reproduced or transmitted in any form or by any means, electronic or mechanical, including photocopying, recording, or any other information storage and retrieval system, without the written permission of the publisher.

Rodale books may be purchased for business or promotional use or for special sales. For information, please write to:
Special Markets Department, Rodale Inc., 733 Third Avenue, New York, NY 10017

Printed in the United States of America
Rodale Inc. makes every effort to use acid-free ♾, recycled paper ♻.

Photo direction by Carol Angstadt
Photographs by Mitch Mandel/Rodale Images
Book design by Amy C. King

Library of Congress Cataloging-in-Publication Data is on file with the publisher.

ISBN 978–1–62336–549–3 hardcover

Distributed to the trade by Macmillan

2 4 6 8 10 9 7 5 3 1 hardcover

RODALE

We inspire and enable people to improve their lives and the world around them.
rodalebooks.com

Author Dawna Stone
Editor Rachel Haugo
Designer Adrian Hardisty-Horsley
Contributing Copy Editor Nancy Dietz
Executive Editor Jill Waage

MEREDITH NATIONAL MEDIA GROUP
President Tom Harty
Senior Vice President, Chief Digital Officer Andy Wilson
Chairman and Chief Executive Officer Stephen M. Lacy
Vice Chairman Mell Meredith Frazier
In Memoriam — E. T. Meredith III (1933-2003)

ISBN 978-0696-30253-4

Photo credits: cover and recipe photos [Dawna Stone], P. 6, 147, 148 [Sheri Kendrick], P. 53, 61, 89 [Karla Konrad], P. 73 [Andy Lyons], P. 79 [Peter Ardito], P. 105, 123 [Jason Donnelly], P. 129 [Blaine Moats].

This publication is intended to provide helpful and informative material and is not intended to treat, diagnose, prevent, or cure any health condition, nor is it intended to replace the advice of a physician. Always consult your physician before adopting a new eating or exercise regimen. The author and publisher specifically disclaim all responsibility for any liability, loss, or risk, personal or otherwise, which is incurred as a consequence of reading or following advice or suggestions in this book.

meredith

© Meredith Corp. 2016. All rights reserved.

As you can see, a lot goes into the formatting of your self-published book. Just remember that you have the opportunity to take advantage of formatting services available on most self-publishing platforms. If you plan to do it on your own, most self-publishing platforms offer well-defined formatting guidelines to follow.

Chapter 14:
A Title That Sells

A strong, catchy book title is almost as important as your cover design. A solid title can mark the difference between a few sales and a bestseller, by helping readers discover your book—and bringing in extra sales with no additional effort.

As you develop your title, use the five tips below to come up with a title that sells. A title should be:

1. Interesting

Your book title should pique the reader's interest. A good title entices people to buy just because of the words on the cover. Leave "boring" behind, and ask yourself: Is this title going to entice the reader to pick up my book?

2. Informative

Your title should help readers understand what they will get out of your book. Fiction pieces experience a bit more leniency when it comes to titles, but since we are talking primarily about nonfiction books, an informative title is important. Don't make a potential reader work hard to figure out the purpose of your book; most likely, they won't take the time to do so. Remember, your title can be made up of two parts—a title and a subtitle. You can get the same benefits by developing a strong and informative subtitle. Including a subtitle that explains the solution or benefits that readers will receive can have the same positive effect as an informative main title.

3. To-the-point

A title that is too lengthy will lose some of its oomph! And a long, drawn-out title will become difficult when designing your cover. Make sure your title is short, sweet and concise. There is no general rule regarding the number of words you should use. Take, for example, the title "Everything You Need to Know About Looking Your Best, Staying Young and Stalling the Aging Process." Wouldn't the title "The Secret to Anti-Aging " be stronger and more to the point? Not to mention, the latter would look much better on a cover! (You could always use the more detailed description for the subtitle.)

4. Marketable or Sales-Focused

If your title and subtitle don't collectively answer these two questions, then they aren't as marketable as they could be.

Q: What is the book about?

Q: What will it do for the reader?

When developing your title, try to come up with a title that answers both questions. If you do this successfully, the title alone will help market the book.

5. Discoverable

Unless you are already famous or have an extensive following, your title can play a large role in readers finding out about your book. Let's be honest, if you're famous, it often doesn't matter what you call your book. If you're Jennifer Aniston, you could title your anti-aging book "The Letter Z," and everyone will know about it. You'll be on the "Today Show," "Good Morning America" and so on. But if you're *not* famous like Jennifer and you name your anti-aging book "The Letter Z," it likely won't get discovered on Amazon and anyone who comes across it would have to dig deeper to find out the subject matter.

Since you want your book to benefit from Amazon or Kindle keywords, think up a title that will sell itself and become easily searchable online. People interested in anti-aging topics will more than likely search on Amazon for "aging" or "anti-aging," and a book titled "The Letter Z" probably won't show up in the search.

Find a title that helps you sell more books—one that is easily discoverable on Amazon.

Once you've come up with a strong title that is interesting, informative, to-the-point, marketable and discoverable, you should do three more quick checks. First, make sure the name's not already taken. Do a general Internet search as well as an Amazon search. Although titles can't be trademarked, it's best to secure a unique title for your book. Second, check to see if the URL is available. Although I don't believe your book necessarily needs its own website—I'm more of a believer in having an author website for all your books or utilizing your company website (if you own your own business)—it could be detrimental to have someone else own and utilize a website matching your book title. Even if you don't plan to develop a website for your book, I suggest purchasing the URL and having it redirect to your author or company page. And thirdly, make sure your title strengthens your book design or at least fits well with the cover's overall look and feel.

If you've followed all the rules in determining a title that sells yet you still want to establish whether you've made the best choice, I suggest testing it. Three simple ways to test your title involve: using your own social media followers and asking them what they think (you can give two options to see which they prefer); finding Facebook groups relevant to your book's topic and creating a poll; or, if you have a small budget, buying some online ads on Google or Facebook. You can create one ad for each title and see which one gets more clicks. (Just make sure your ads are targeted toward the appropriate audience.)

Remember, if you're self-publishing your book, you can always tweak your title even after you publish. But if you follow the advice above, you should immediately have a title that sells!

Chapter 15:
A Cover That Captivates

You will sell more books with a great cover design than you will with a poor design, no matter how great your book's content. Some may even say that your cover proves more important than your content; without a great cover to capture your readers, you'll be less likely to get that amazing content into others' hands.

A book cover is also an important part of your marketing. A dynamic cover can help market your book, whereas a poor cover can very likely hamper your efforts. Follow these tips to design a cover that captivates your potential readers.

A book cover that captivates is one that:

1) **Connects with your audience**: Your cover design needs to attract your specific readership. A book on training puppies shouldn't look like a suspense or

horror novel, while a book exploring rocket science shouldn't appear to be an organic gardening book. Make sure your cover appropriately represents your content and attracts your specific target audience.

2) **Is eye-catching**: Use fonts, colors, images and/or graphics that make your book stand out. And keep it simple. Too much design on a cover can become distracting. The most eye-catching covers make a statement—subtly.

3) **Is designed professionally**: Investing in a professionally-designed cover is absolutely imperative, as readers almost always judge a book by its cover. Remember, your book cover not only represents your work, but it also speaks to you and your business. If done correctly, your reader should not be able to tell the difference between your self-published book and one that was designed by a large publishing company.

4) **Converts well to a smaller size or thumbnail**: Make sure your book cover converts well when shrunken to thumbnail size. These days most people won't find your book on the bookstore shelf, so you have to consider how they will see it—likely as a thumbnail on Amazon, slightly bigger in your online marketing, a quarter of the actual size in your email blasts, etc. Make sure the most important elements stand out when viewed in a smaller size.

5) **Helps convey your message**: Your cover should reflect the topic of your book. The reader should be able to discern the book's genre by simply glimpsing at the cover. One main element often proves more effective than several.

If you're a professional graphic designer, then you should be able to design your own impactful cover; however, if you're not, I recommend leaving it to the professionals.

A professional cover doesn't have to break the bank. In fact, some great design sites can offer multiple cover options relatively inexpensively. I've heard a lot of positive feedback about 99designs, and I've used crowdSPRING for several projects. I've also used a professional designer. The choice is yours. If you use a contest design site like 99designs or crowdSPRING, you can get upward of 40 or more cover options for as little as $250 to $300. A designer could cost your anywhere between $300 and $1,000, depending on his or her skill level and the complexity of your cover.

Whether you use a contest site or an individual, the first step should always be developing a design brief. This vision for your cover will be utilized by whomever designs it. To come up with your concept, I suggest looking online at other bestselling covers in your genre and by browsing bookstore shelves. Notice what you like and dislike and what stands out or grabs your attention. Use this research to come up with your brief, which simply provides the designer with some background on your book and thoughts regarding the direction they should take in terms of colors, images and other aesthetic factors. You can also provide them with cover samples from other books you like. This will give everyone involved a better feel for exactly what you're looking for.

Don't forget about the back cover and the spine, too; both are crucial elements of your book cover. The back cover is where you sell not only your book, but also yourself as the author. Make sure you use this valuable real estate to sufficiently entice readers to buy the product. When done right, a book cover—front, spine and back—should leave a lasting impression.

Once your cover has been designed or you've narrowed down your top picks, you'll benefit yet again from asking for feedback, much like the process I mentioned in Chapter 11. Use the same three testing options for your cover as we discussed for your title in the previous chapter. When seeking feedback from followers, I've found that giving no more than three options works best. Ask participants to pick their favorite and to provide a brief reason for their selection.

I used this simple polling method to help choose the cover of my cookbook. My publisher and I had been fluctuating between two different options. We weren't sure which one to go with and, although I liked both covers, I felt slightly stronger about one and my publisher felt slightly stronger about the other. So we took it to my social media followers (90,000-plus strong at the time). Not only did we get an overwhelming response—I have never received more comments on a single post—but a clear winner emerged. The publisher took the feedback to heart and printed the book with the cover that my fans wanted.

Publish

Chapter 16:
Self-Publishing vs. Traditional Publishing

There are advantages and disadvantages to both self publishing and traditional publishing. I've been fortunate to have books published both ways.

Hachette Book Group (HBG) published my business success book. HBG is a division of the third largest trade and educational book publisher in the world, Hachette Livre. With the help of a literary agent and a well-written book proposal, I was able to land my very first book deal and receive a five-figure advance in the process.

My second book, a health and wellness book, was my first self-published work. I wrote the book in less than 12 weeks and used CreateSpace for both the print and e-book versions. Book sales did so well that I received interest from several large publishers, and I was able to garner a six-figure book deal to expand on the original book from powerhouse wellness publisher Rodale Books. That book, my third, was a full color, 200-plus-page cookbook called "The Healthy You Diet."

My fourth book, another wellness book, was neither self-published nor traditionally published. It was published in partnership with Meredith Corporation and "Shape" magazine.

I have been fortunate to experience several different ways an author can publish a book, and I've learned many things in the process.

I can honestly say that one method isn't better than the other. In fact, each offers its own set of pros and cons. As the author, you just need to decide what works best for you and your end goal. Sometimes that decision is made for you. For example, my second book, the one I self-published, was only self-published because I couldn't get a publisher to give me a deal. It received rejections again and again. Yet instead of shelving the idea, I decide to try my hand at self-publishing. I felt passionate about the book, and I believed there was an audience for it, so I moved forward on my own. The book did so well that the same publishers who said they weren't interested in my self-published book, were now taking meetings with my agent and me.

Many people dream about getting a big book deal with a large advance. Although it's an amazing experience that often includes photo shoots and national media exposure, it's not always easy to land a traditional book deal. Fortunately, self-publishing is no longer frowned upon; in fact, self-publishing can be a better avenue for many, especially for a first-time author. The next two chapters take a look at the pros and cons of self-publishing versus traditional publishing. Find out what's best for you.

Chapter 17:
Self-Publishing

Self-publishing is the way to go for most first-time authors. It's simple, it's quick, and it gives you complete control over your product. Here are some of the pros and cons:

Pros:

- Uncomplicated
- Short lead time
- Full ownership/copyright of your work
- Complete control of your schedule
- You calling all the shots
- Higher profits from book sales
- Inexpensive to publish with today's tools

Cons:

- No advance
- Need to hire your own editor
- Need to design and format your own book cover and interior pages
- No outside marketing support
- Typically no bookstore sales

If you're using your book as a tool to build your business, boost your career or get noticed in your industry, then self-publishing remains a great option. But if you have your heart set on getting a publishing deal and an advance for your book, it's worth looking into the traditional publishing process. Just remember, 12 publishers rejected JK Rowling before she received a book deal for her "Harry Potter" series. You may go through many rejections before you find a publisher who wants to work with you. But the beauty of today's world? You have countless other options—self-publishing being a great one.

Now that you know the pros and cons of self-publishing, let's look at traditional publishing, too.

> **Self-Publishing Tip:**
>
> *If you are going to self-publish your book, it is best to have both a print version and a kindle/e-book version available, as having both will improve your Amazon ranking.*

Chapter 18:
Traditional Publishing

Although self-publishing has become much more mainstream and many extremely successful authors have emerged from the process, publishing with a large publisher still holds a certain a level of clout. And although the media is rapidly changing and putting self-published authors on air, some of the big national shows still steer clear of self-published book authors unless they have received overwhelming notoriety.

Let's look at the traditional publisher route's pros and cons.

Pros:

- Possible advance
- Marketing support
- Graphic/design support
- Bookstore distribution

Cons:

- Long lead time (can take more than a year to publish your book)
- No or little control over your book design
- Publisher owning the copyright
- Difficulty in getting accepted by a publisher
- Often the necessity to write a book proposal
- Often the necessity for an agent to get you in the door/land a deal
- Only receiving a small portion of sales—often as little as $1 per book

I contemplated listing many more pros under the traditional publishing process, but times have changes; having a traditional publisher no longer guarantees additional marketing or PR. And although it may be easier to get national TV or radio coverage with a traditionally-published book, that too has changed drastically over the past few years. Gone are the days when a publisher could guarantee media coverage for a book.

If you're still leaning toward attempting a traditional book deal, you will most likely need to write a formal book proposal. To date, I have written three book proposals, all of which have sold—one to HBG as mentioned above, one to Rodale Inc. (the publisher of well-known books like "The South Beach Diet," "The Atkins Diet" and "Wheat Belly," plus popular magazines like "Women's Health," "Men's Health" and "Prevention") and one to Meredith Corp., which owns a vast number of popular magazines including "Shape," "Better Homes & Gardens," "Allrecipes," "Parents" and "EatingWell."

Both large publishing houses told me that my book proposal is what caught their attention. One of my editors even deemed it one of the best she had ever seen.

I know that most of you reading this book more than likely plan to self-publish your book. And although I've taken both routes, I still believe self-publishing is the best option for most first-time authors. If, however, you still have your heart set on trying to get a traditional book deal, I've made available (for free) my "How to Write a Six-Figure Book Proposal." Simply go to www.BookAccelerator.com to download your free copy.

Even if you plan to self-publish, you may want to download this free ebook, as some of the elements included in writing a great proposal can help you with the planning process for your self-published book. Added bonus: It also shares the number one secret to getting a deal! This is something I used in all three of my proposals—and something you won't want to miss.

Market

Chapter 19:
Building Pre-Launch Buzz

How you go about building pre-launch buzz will depend on your current following or author platform. That is, if you already have a large social media following, blog reader base or email list, your ability to create pre-launch buzz will be much easier than if you're starting from scratch. At a minimum, you'll need a website or web landing page, a social media presence and an email list. Let's look at each of these tools and how we use them to build pre-launch buzz.

Small or non-existent author platform:

If you don't currently have a following, you will need to determine how you want to reach potential readers. At the minimum, I would suggest using at least one social media platform like Facebook, some email marketing and a simple website or page on a current website.

Social Media

Pick one or two social media platforms with which you feel most comfortable. Some good platforms for authors include Facebook, Instagram, Twitter and Pinterest. I mostly use Facebook and Instagram. If you don't use any social media now, I suggest picking just one platform to focus on. Set up your account, and start posting content that relates to your book. If you're just beginning, I don't expect you to spend hours on social media; however, since we will be using some social media advertising to promote your book, you will want to have some pre-populated posts so it isn't obvious you're just getting started.

Once you pre-populate your chosen social media platform with good content, you should spend a small amount of money on advertising to build a following for your book. When I launched my cookbook, I ran a few "likes" ads on Facebook that simply utilized one of my recipe photos (a quinoa salad) with text that said "Like page for more healthy recipes like this quinoa salad." This enabled me to build a following of people I knew were interested in healthy recipes—my book's core demographic. I knew most of my potential readers would be women aged 24 to 54, so I promoted my ad only to this group.

You don't have to spend a ton of money to build an initial following. I like using a daily budget for a set number of days, i.e. $5 a day for 20 days. I usually test two different ads to see which one does better. I keep the same copy but test two different images to see which one resonates with my audience. If you run both ads in the same campaign, Facebook will automatically run the ad that gets better results (i.e. the most clicks).

Friends and Family Email Marketing

Even if you don't have a large social media following or an email database of fans, you most likely have a list of friends, family and co-workers who can help build your base of future followers. Let your social media platform send out a notice to your contacts informing them that you now subscribe to that particular platform. Also clean up your email lists of friends and family making sure your addresses are up-to-date, as we will be using both your social media following and email list to build buzz.

The best way to get people excited about your future book is to get them involved in the process. And the best way to do that? Ask for others' opinions. Poll your social media fans and those individuals you have emails for about their thoughts on possible titles, subtitles and even cover designs. As I mentioned earlier, when I published my cookbook, we couldn't decide between two cover designs. I put both covers on my social media platforms and asked my friends/fans for their thoughts. The response was incredible; everyone likes to share an opinion. I also emailed my friends and family and asked for their input. Not only did I get great feedback, but I now had a large group of people aware of my book—even without me trying to promote it to them. It's a win-win.

Website

Having a website proves important if you want to build your email list. You don't, however, need a complicated or robust site (or even a dedicated website) for your book. A simple scrolling, one-page WordPress site can be sufficient or even a page on a website that's already in existence. If you already have a company website or a personal author website, I wouldn't suggest building another. You do not need a unique website for your book; in fact, I usually discourage it. Simply having a web page where you can capture emails as email marketing will prove the number one way to promote sales of your book.

Use Lead Magnets

So how do you capture email addresses if you don't already have a robust following? You need to provide people with something of value for free. This is often called a "lead magnet." It can be an article, a quiz or even an entire book (if you've written several). If your "giveaway" carries value, people will be willing to provide their email addresses in exchange for the free e-delivery. The people who sign up to receive your "gift" then become your potential customers and readers.

Think about something you can give away that is directly related to your book. For example, while writing *Book Accelerator*, I originally included an entire chapter on writing a six-figure book proposal. Yet when I was editing the book, that chapter didn't seem to fit, given that the bulk of the content focuses on self-publishing. So I decided to pull out the chapter, expand on the topic and provide an entire ebook on the subject as one of my lead magnets. This allowed me to provide something of value to my readers while building my email database of people interested in writing a book.

Think about what you have to offer your potential reader or client. Make sure it is of value, and use it to build an even more robust email list—one that you can use to market your book and business.

In order to capture emails you will need to have a place where people can download your giveaway, or have an email autoresponder like AWeber, Convertkit or Infusionsoft to help you manage the process. An entire book could be written on this subject. And although this book doesn't aim to teach you how to build a website or utilize an email autoresponder, I do want to provide a high-level overview so you have sufficient knowledge to know what to research and what to follow up on. Then you can decide how far you want to go.

For some of you, it will be enough simply having a book to give potential clients or to use as your calling card. For others, you may want to launch a robust marketing campaign that includes social media, email marketing and other tools. Take the time to research email autoresponders, and select the option that works best given your unique needs.

If you already have a large author platform, you are one step ahead of the game and simply need a pre-launch plan to best take advantage of your network. Ask your followers for their input on titles, subtitles, cover options and other items. When reaching out to my lists in the past, I've even gone so far as to ask my nearly 100,000 fans which author photo I should use on the back of my book. And although I loved getting great feedback, even better was letting all my fans know about my upcoming book without having to sell them. Asking for their opinion was well received and allowed for engagement before I even began book sales.

Once you are set up on social media and have consolidated email lists, a working website or web page and an up-and-running email autoresponder, you are ready to build out a robust marketing program. In the next chapter, I'll share with you the exact plan I used for my first self-published book—the one that quickly hit the bestseller list and earned me a six-figure book deal.

Chapter 20:
Launching Your Book

In this chapter, I share with you the exact marketing plan I used to launch my first self-published book, "Healthy You." The book did so well that I was able to land a traditional book deal based on my self-published book sales. I do want to note that—by no means—must you do everything on this list to be successful. In fact, many extremely successful self-published authors only focus on one or two marketing techniques, like email marketing or Facebook ads. Do what works best for you, and remember that it's better to do one or two things really well than to do many things poorly.

Although I did many of the items on the plan, some things admittedly slipped through the cracks; other items started off strong and didn't maintain the same momentum. For example, the plan calls for two to four blog posts a week. In truth, I started off strongly, but over the first few weeks,

I became more likely to only post once or twice per week. As the weeks went by, one post per week became more of the norm.

As you review my plan, remember to concentrate your efforts on the tasks that make the most sense for you. I learned very quickly that some items on my marketing plan felt like a waste of time while others guaranteed a home run. But I wouldn't have known which things resonated with my potential readers had I not given them a shot. For example, my blog posts took me a long time to compose, but they didn't really move the needle. Guest blogging, however, proved a huge success. I was invited to write some posts for a few well-known websites. These posts— directly related to my book—helped promote my work. One guest post did so well that I sold six times more books the week the post was published than any previous week.

Use my marketing plan as a guide, but tailor it to your needs based on your audience and what your own schedule allows. When I implemented the plan below, I had just sold my company and had more free time than ever before. Since then, I have launched two new companies and become extremely busy, so I too would need to tailor the plan, given the amount of time and effort now available to put into a new book launch.

Online Book Promotion Plan

AUTHOR WEBSITE AND BLOG

Maintain an active, fresh website with constant updates. (Website should be updated daily or weekly.)

Website: Readers

1) Establish relationship with "Healthy You!" readers. Offer a forum so that readers can communicate with the author and get their questions answered.

2) Offer readers additional information outside of "Healthy You!":

   a) Additional bonus recipes

   b) Food images

   c) Specific ingredient information

   d) Photos of reader recipes

   e) Testimonials

   f) Blog posts

   g) Forums

   h) How-to videos

   i) Etc.

Website: Non-Readers

1) Offer enough information about the book for non-readers to be pulled in and ultimately buy the book.

Blog

1) Create at least 2-4 new blog entries per week.
2) Host 'guest blogs' from related professionals and readers.
3) Include lots of photos in each blog post to engage interest.
4) Topics can be centered around bonus recipes, nutritional information, new data and statistics related to healthy eating, the health food industry, documentaries, books/author interviews, healthy living articles, author experiences, etc.
    a) Should be able to link to other social media avenues as often as possible.

EMAIL MARKETING

Create email campaigns promoting the book and/or book signings to local and national distribution lists.

Distribution Lists:

1) Friends and family
2) Companies and organizations that we have worked with previously

Partnerships

1) Inclusion in partners' newsletters and email campaigns

SOCIAL NETWORKING AND SOCIAL MEDIA

Facebook

1) Connect with anyone interested in healthy cooking/wholesome eating/weight loss.
2) Incorporate the following:

   a) Personal sharing (photos, updates, etc.)

   b) Photos!

   c) Recipes

   d) News articles

   e) Inspirational messages

   f) Questions

   g) Giveaways

3) Post 1 to 3 times per day.
4) Connect Facebook and Instagram to Twitter.

Instagram

1) Focus on food photos.

2) Photograph everything related to healthy eating and cooking.

3) 90% of all uploads should relate to healthy eating/cooking.

Twitter

1) Continue to build Twitter following.
    a) Provide informative content.
    b) Provide links to recipes and recent blog posts or articles.

2) Prior to the book's launch, follow a minimum of 25 new people a day (those related to cooking, healthy eating and weight loss).

Pinterest

1) Continue to build a presence on Pinterest—especially focusing on the most popular boards i.e. clean and healthy recipes.

2) Develop a new board for "Healthy You!"

LinkedIn

1) Continue to use LinkedIn as a tool to connect with industry leaders, TV producers, radio personalities, etc.

YouTube

1) Continue to expand YouTube presence by uploading 2-4 new videos a month.

OTHER BLOGS

1) Virtual book tours
2) Author interviews on top healthy eating, cooking or weight loss blogs
3) Book giveaways
4) Guest blogging

AUDIO AND VIDEO PROMOTIONS

1) Video introducing the book and premise for Amazon author page.
2) Host videos on website.
   a) Release 2-4 videos per month.
   b) Set schedule to shoot up to 10 (60- 90-second) videos.

        i) Welcome/intro to "Healthy You!"

        ii) Prepare your pantry

        iii) How-to videos for each recipe

    c) Encourage readers to send in videos as they prepare the recipes.

3) YouTube Channel

    a) Continue to build YouTube following and post 2-4 new videos per month.

PROMOTIONAL GIVEAWAYS/CONTESTS

1) Launch promotional book giveaways via social media and popular blogs.

2) Host giveaways (promotional items, non-book related) on book's website/blog/social media to draw people into the page and to be 'liked'.

ONLINE ADVERTISING

1) Target women interested in health, wellness, cooking, clean eating and weight loss.

    a) Facebook – daily ads following book release

I realize the marketing plan I shared is extremely robust. And although it proved successful for me, some items worked much better than others given my unique situation (like my volume of social media followers, etc.). I did, however, want to provide you with the entire plan as initially developed—without any edits or changes.

Assess your own strengths and weaknesses as you determine your plan. I know many authors who would benefit tremendously from blogging, but I just can't get myself to do it. Likewise, although the plan called for two to four videos on YouTube a month, I only did this during the launch—an approximately three-month period. As you build out a marketing plan for your book, use my scheme as a starting point from which to pull ideas. Also, make sure you don't bite off more than you can chew.

The marketing plan I shared above allowed me to make Amazon's bestseller list within the first week of my book launch, and I did this without any discounted pricing—something that most self-published authors must do in order to make the list. I'm sharing this because I want you to understand that there are multiple ways to hit the bestseller list. One way involves implementing a stellar marketing plan that gets the book noticed and drives sales. The other is to deeply discount your book during the launch phase. Some authors even provide their book for free for several weeks to get more people to download, read and review it.

The reason I didn't deeply discount my self-published book during its launch had nothing to do with how I felt about price manipulation. In fact, I had no idea at the time that many authors use this strategy to get noticed, frontload sales and increase Amazon rankings. The good thing about not knowing this? I was forced to develop a marketing plan so robust that it alone drove book sales and, in turn, rank. It also taught me that combining these two strategies (marketing and pricing) can be a surefire way to hit the bestsellers list. So how do you best combine these two strategies?

Build out a strong marketing plan using the tips and suggestions provided above, and combine that with a deeply discounted price for a finite period of time. For example, price your e-book at 99 cents for the first three to five days of its launch. Then focus all your marketing on promoting this offer. Initiate email campaigns, post about it on social media, and focus on online advertising, video promotions, etc. Use all your marketing tactics to get the word out about the 99-cent offer.

Kindle Direct Publishing (KDP) offers a program called KDP Select. KDP Select offers you the ability to do countdown deals and free promotions. The program does however call for exclusivity and has many rules. There have recently been some changes to KDP Select but you can always find the current rules on the KDP website.

If done well, the combination of your marketing and discounted pricing can guarantee that you become a bestseller. Making the bestsellers list will then provide even more promotion and discoverability for your book, helping you to sell more copies when you increase your price.

I discuss pricing as well as KDP Select in greater detail in the Book Accelerator online course. You can find out more at BookAccelerator.com

Take the time needed to plan both your marketing strategy and pricing structure. If you then utilize your marketing to promote the discounted pricing, your chances of reaching the bestsellers list will rise exponentially!

Monetize

Chapter 21:
Monetize Your Book

If you own a business, then your book can help build it by providing leads, generating recognition and giving you credibility—all benefits that translate to more revenue and profits. If, however, you are also looking to develop some additional income streams beyond growing your business, your book can expose you to many other potential moneymaking endeavors. People often think that authors get rich off their book sales, but, in fact, most authors make the bulk of their money on other (non-book sales) opportunities that come along with being a published author.

The most common income producers for authors include:

- Speaking engagements
- Blogging (ad sales)
- Affiliate partnerships

- Product sales based on your book
- Seminars
- Coaching/consulting
- Online courses
- Podcasting
- Radio show
- Subscriber-based newsletter
- Guest posting

I'm sure there are other possibilities I'm missing. I'm always amazed at the creative business concepts that authors come up with to leverage book sales. The important thing to remember is that your book opens doors and provides opportunities that didn't exist prior to being a published author.

Many ways exist to monetize your book beyond sales, but rather than attempting them all, do what you do best. If you dread organizing even small events like birthday, anniversary or office parties, then putting on a large in-person seminar may not be for you. On the other hand, an online seminar might be right up your alley.

Similarly, if talking in front of a large group gives you severe anxiety, then becoming a professional speaker might not be the best way to monetize your book. Over the years,

I've been able to figure out what I enjoy and what's just not for me. I found rather quickly that I don't enjoy blogging. I want to, but I just can't get myself to do it. I always find that I gravitate toward working on my current book rather than writing another blog post. I have, however, found some pleasure in writing guest posts for other blogs. I've written online posts—some paid and some done for free to promote my book—for mindbodygreen, "Prevention" magazine, Well + Good, "Shape" magazine, "Fitness" magazine and many more.

My main source of book income outside of direct book sales has come through speaking engagements. The first few talks I gave—my first nearly 18 years ago—I did for free. Today I get up to $10,000 for an hour-long talk (with a discount given to nonprofit organizations), and I rarely ever do free speaking engagements. To date, I've probably done well over 50 talks, spread out across the country. I've done speaking engagements or been on panel discussions for The PGA Tour, Women's Entertainment Television, Wharton School of Business, Chobani, American Heart Association, Disney, the Super Bowl Leadership Forum and many others.

Look back at the list of author opportunities now, and determine which ones interest you. Then take advantage of them. Launch a podcast or seminar, let companies and organizations know you're available for speaking engagements, or join a speaker's bureau. Develop a membership site with a coveted newsletter, coach, consult, or develop a product around your book. The opportunities are endless.

Find which opportunities are best for you and reap the financial benefits of being an author!

Conclusion

Chapter 22:
Accountability

As I mentioned earlier, I've written four best-selling books. I wrote my first book, a 60,000-word book, in less than 16 weeks, my second and third books, both 40,000-plus words in under 12 weeks and my fourth book, a 30,000-word book, in under 6 weeks!

I received a five-figure book deal for my first book, I self-published my second one, and I received a six-figure deal for my third book. (Both advances came from large, well-known publishing houses.) My fourth book was published in partnership with "Shape" magazine.

I'm reminding you of this again because, prior to landing my first book deal, I spent nearly 20 years trying to write a book. Yes, 20 years! I would start writing and gain momentum for a few days, only to get busy or distracted before pushing the project aside. It wasn't that I lacked the passion for writing a book; I just never seemed to be able to make writing a priority.

The reason I finally completed my first book wasn't because I suddenly found the time; it was because I received a book deal. An agent convinced me to write a book proposal and "shop" it around in search of interest. When Hachette Book Group (HBG), one of the "big five" publishing companies along with Holtzbrinck/Macmillian, Penguin Random House, HarperCollins and Simon & Schuster, gave me a five-figure book deal, I no longer had any excuses for procrastinating. In fact, procrastination was no longer an option. I now had a strict deadline that I needed to adhere to. This accountability helped (or I should say forced) me to make my book writing a priority and to set a writing schedule I had to adhere to in order to meet my deadlines.

Getting a book deal isn't an easy task and, honestly, it may not be the best option for everyone. But for me, getting a book deal provided accountability—something I found to be invaluable when finishing my first book. Without set deadlines or a process and timeline to follow, finishing a book can feel nearly impossible. The deadline imposed by my publisher led me to follow through, while forcing me to implement a system for writing consistently. That system became the *Book Accelerator* methodology. It's this framework that has allowed me to successfully finish every book I've started—even when I didn't have deadlines imposed by my publisher. *Book Accelerator* provides a framework to follow that quickly takes you from idea to finished book!

For some of you, this book will be all you need to go from topic inception to completed book. For others, you may still feel that you need further motivation to get you through the process. If that is the case, I have two additional ways to help you reach the finish line. First, find an accountability partner; second, follow an online course that can walk you through the process and keep you motivated and on track. Let's look at both options:

Find an Accountability Partner

An accountability partner is someone who you check in with on a regular basis to provide additional support and to keep you motivated during the process.

This person can be a spouse, friend, co-worker or even another author. The ideal accountability partner will be someone who:

- Wants to see you succeed
- Is positive and energetic
- Provides praise and support

- Has your best interest at heart
- Will be tough but shows compassion

Most importantly, he or she will provide that additional motivation you need to keep moving forward with your writing.

Join Book Accelerator University

If you can't find an accountability partner or you feel like you may need even more formal support, you should consider joining my Book Accelerator University, a 16-week online course. I don't want this to sound like a marketing pitch, as I'm already so grateful that you took the time to read my book and will hopefully find success on your journey to becoming a published author. But as a mom of two young kids and the owner of two businesses, I know that an online course can give you that extra motivation needed to follow through. The *Book Accelerator* course will take you step by step through the book writing and marketing processes, and the seven modules and 41 videos will help you:

- Perfect your vision and concept
- Determine your audience
- Find your voice
- Convey the problem and solution in a way that intrigues your reader

- Develop a book structure that works
- Write a killer introduction
- Capture the reader's attention
- Use Mind Mapping and Diamond Mapping™ to build your detailed outline
- Build successful writing habits
- Make the editing process a smooth one
- Develop a title that sells
- Create a cover that captivates!
- Build buzz for your launch
- Market your book
- Monetize your book
- Hit the bestseller list!

Each module has been designed to take you, step by step, through the Book Accelerator methodology. Each video provides clear and concise information to help you not only keep up the momentum but also to once again make writing fun. The online course also includes bonus articles to aid your progress.

If you're struggling to finish or even start your book, following the Book Accelerator methodology can help. If you have an extremely busy schedule and feel like you need to be personally walked through each step, the Book

Accelerator online course is for you! You can learn more and view the course curriculum at www.BookAccelerator.com

The Book Accelerator methodology is a proven process to get you from idea to finished book in less than 16 weeks. If you're motivated to write your book, the Book Accelerator online course provides the additional accountability needed to push past time constraints and to make your writing a priority. Don't let anything hold you back from your dream of becoming an author. It's time to write a book that will boost your business or career, increase your income and get you noticed!

Don't waste another moment. Get started today!

Let me personally walk you through the process and ensure your book is done in 16 weeks!

Take the next step…

JOIN THE BOOK ACCELERATOR ONLINE COURSE!

7 modules and more than 30 lessons

Find out more at BookAccelerator.com

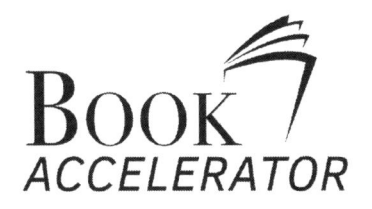

Appendix I: Self-Publishing Resources

Although I'd love for this book to provide every single detail you need to know about self-publishing, there are simply too many items to cover them all. I've included below some of the tools, software and other resources that I've either used myself or have heard positive feedback about. I hope these resources help you find the best service or process to use along your self-publishing journey.

Email autoresponders

- Convertkit
- AWeber
- Infusionsoft
- ActiveCampaign
- MailChimp

Website Platforms

- WordPress

Design Services
- 99designs
- CrowdSPRING
- Archangel Ink

Self-publishing platforms
- CreateSpace
- Kindle Direct Publishing
- IngramSpark

Editing services
- CreateSpace
- Kindle Direct Publishing
- Upwork
- Fiverr

How to Write a Book Proposal
- www.BookAccelerator.com

Polling Services/Software
- SurveyMonkey
- PickFu

Appendix II: Sample Focus Group Invite Letter

Dear _____

As you may know, I am in the process of writing my second book, a healthy eating/weight loss book. As I finalize the manuscript, I am looking for a small group of people to share their thoughts and provide feedback on the book.

We are interested in your opinion and would personally like to invite you to join a focus group on Wednesday, April 3, from 6 to 7:30 p.m. at the Renaissance Vinoy Resort. (Conference room will be provided shortly.)

If you would like to be part of the focus group, we will provide you with a draft of the manuscript by Wednesday, March 20, giving you two full weeks to read the book.

Although this is a weight loss book, the main topic focuses on clean, healthy eating. The target audience is both people who want to lose weight as well as those who just want to eat healthier. We are looking for input from people who relate to either goal.

If you are interested in attending, please read and sign the attached confidentiality agreement and email a copy to Ellen at [email]. We will contact you and schedule the delivery of the manuscript.

If you have any questions, please do not hesitate to ask. Also, if you have a friend or family member who may be interested in joining the group, too, please have them contact us.

We look forward to hearing back from you.

Sincerely,

Dawna Stone

To my valued readers,

Thank you for taking time to read *Book Accelerator*. I'm confident if you follow the step-by-step process, you can publish your book in less than 16 weeks!

As an author or future author you probably know how important it is to get positive reviews for your book. I would be so thankful if you could take a minute and provide an honest review for this book. **Thank you so much!**

To your author success!

Dawna Stone

Made in the USA
Columbia, SC
08 November 2017